G000153961

Virtual a
Networked
Organizations

Philippa Collins

- Fast track route to understanding the scope and variety of virtual organizations, and the impact of information and communications technologies on the way we do business

- Covers the key areas of virtual organizations, from using Internet and wireless technologies to streamline your supply chain and working practices to e-learning and adapting your management style to meet the new challenges

- Examples and lessons from some of the world's most successful businesses, including Lands' End, HSBC, Manugistics and BT, and ideas from the smartest thinkers, including Eddie Obeng, Jessica Lipnack and Jeffrey Stamps

- Includes a glossary of key concepts and a comprehensive resources guide

essential management thinking at your fingertips

The right of Philippa Collins to be identified as the author of this work has been asserted in accordance with the Copyright, Designs and Patents Act 1988

First published 2002 by
Capstone Publishing (a Wiley company)
8 Newtec Place
Magdalen Road
Oxford OX4 1RE
United Kingdom
http://www.capstoneideas.com

CIP catalogue records for this book are available from the British Library and the US Library of Congress

ISBN 1-84112-220-3

Printed and bound in Great Britain

This book is printed on acid-free paper

Substantial discounts on bulk quantities of Capstone books are available to corporations, professional associations and other organizations. Please contact Capstone for more details on +44 (0)1865 798 623 or (fax) +44 (0)1865 240 941 or (e-mail) info@wiley-capstone.co.uk

Contents

Introduction to ExpressExec

ExpressExec is 3 million words of the latest management thinking compiled into 10 modules. Each module contains 10 individual titles forming a comprehensive resource of current business practice written by leading practitioners in their field. From brand management to balanced scorecard, ExpressExec enables you to grasp the key concepts behind each subject and implement the theory immediately. Each of the 100 titles is available in print and electronic formats.

Through the ExpressExec.com Website you will discover that you can access the complete resource in a number of ways:

» printed books or e-books;
» e-content – PDF or XML (for licensed syndication) adding value to an intranet or Internet site;
» a corporate e-learning/knowledge management solution providing a cost-effective platform for developing skills and sharing knowledge within an organization;
» bespoke delivery – tailored solutions to solve your need.

Why not visit www.expressexec.com and register for free key management briefings, a monthly newsletter and interactive skills checklists. Share your ideas about ExpressExec and your thoughts about business today.

Please contact elound@wiley-capstone.co.uk for more information.

Introduction: Why Go Virtual?

Going virtual is a question of survival. In an accelerating world, organizations need to use every means available to maximize relationships with their stakeholders. Three long-term options are suggested.

» Do nothing.
» Dominate.
» Evolve into a virtual organization.

''Most of us don't work with the rest of us.''
Comment from Shell Expo workshop 2001

Going virtual is not about technology; it is about new forms of management. Empowered by the information and communications technologies, we can reinvent the way we work in new and exciting ways. ''Business as usual'' is obsolete!

Why is this topic so important? Ask yourself:

» Do I want to be competitive?
» Do I want to be innovative and creative?
» Do I want my business to survive?

If the answer to these questions is ''yes,'' you need to understand ''virtual.'' Before you can start, you need to see the bigger picture of the business environment. That is, you have to share a fundamental belief that the business environment is significantly different from what it was 10–15 years ago. It is obvious that the pace of change is getting faster. People are finding that it is not just one step change as they once thought, but it is never-ending. We also need to understand that change is driven not just by technology, but also by things like legislation, which is accelerating as all countries are trying to catch up to achieve compatibility across borders.

In an accelerating world, how do organizations cope with this change? Their learning cannot catch up. Eddie Obeng has written about this in his book *New Rules for the New World*.[1] We started in a world where you can learn faster than the rate of change. Now we cannot keep up. Our ability and *willingness* to change and the *capacity* to change, to learn, and to evolve are slack. Eddie Obeng suggests that as we are evolving from the ''Old World'' to the ''New World,'' there are three long-term options:

1 *Don't do anything*. Chill out! Your systems will get out of date; people will get demoralized; you will have to keep reorganizing to keep up with the market; this will cost money, so you need new capital. Eventually you will die.
2 *Dominate*. This is the route most organizations take. They think that if they get really big they will not have to change. This led to merger mania. It leads to globalization and megaglobal organizations.

If the environment is changing faster than you can manage, and you double in size, will that help you go faster? Unfortunately, you will probably move more slowly. So the strategy has to be, dominate so that you do not have to change – you think you can survive as long as you can dictate to your customers.

3 *Evolve and match the new environment*. Go virtual, so that you have the effect of being a large organization without the traditional form or the hassles of a bureaucratic organization.

Understanding *Virtual and Networked Organizations* involves a tour of astonishing variety. Virtual organizations come in many shapes and sizes. There is no typical case, and the text is based on examples from many organizations to illustrate this point.

Fitting the various topics into the ExpressExec format was quite a challenge! It has been difficult to decide which elements to include, and which to leave out. We are not producing an encyclopedia, so we can be selective. You may not entirely agree with the choices made, but there just is not space to cover every aspect. After discussing different interpretations of the concepts in Chapter 2, there is an introduction to some of the changes in management thought in Chapter 3. In Chapter 4 we draw attention to the development of self-service models, illustrating this change with three diverse case studies. The "e" factor is further illustrated in Chapter 5, which focuses on the links between e-business and globalization.

Chapter 6 gives an introduction to some of the exciting technologies that support virtual working, and have the potential to further change the way we work. Chapter 7 demonstrates successful use of the new concepts by two large companies – Lands' End and HSBC. There are also excellent case studies illustrating changing work practices and the way it is possible to implement a completely new business model. Key management concepts that underpin virtual organizations are addressed in Chapter 8, and some of the resources available for further study are collected in Chapter 9. The final chapter stresses the need to understand change management and for a well-developed strategy for "going virtual," and offers useful guidelines for implementation.

I hope you enjoy this review of our changing business world. The aim is to describe in broad outline the impact and potential of virtual organizations, with specific emphasis on management and behavioral issues. The war against terrorism has altered perceptions even during the preparation of this text. With so much more insecurity and fear in the world, virtual working could become even more important. I am assuming an optimistic stance. I am constantly astonished at the vigor and effectiveness of online interactions.[2] The stories in this text bear further witness to the power of networking and virtual organization.

KEY ISSUES EXAMINED IN THIS TEXT

» Working virtually and networking are not new phenomena.
» Telecommunications technologies have given us the potential to work in new ways and to structure our businesses in new ways.
» Virtual organizations range in scope from *ad hoc* teams to total businesses.
» In an accelerating world, we need to rethink our perceptions of organization and management.

NOTES

1 Obeng, E. (1997) *New Rules for the New World*. Capstone. (www.pentaclethevbs.com).
2 For an interesting personal account, read Rheingold, H. (1994) *The Virtual Community*. Secker & Warburg. Although this is dated in parts, it still offers an excellent overview.

Defining Virtual and Networked Organizations

The scope of virtual and networked organizations is wide-ranging. Here different interpretations are introduced, together with basic concepts and key factors.

» Time and location (24 × 7).
» Levels of involvement.
» Management issues.

"As a net is made up of a series of ties, so everything in this world is connected by a series of ties. If anyone thinks that this mesh of a net is an independent, isolated thing, he is mistaken. It is called a net because it is made up of a series of interconnected meshes, and each mesh has its place and responsibility in relation to other meshes."

Buddha

Not surprisingly, no simple definition will cover the whole of this subject. There is a growing literature and much hype concerning the issues and trends in virtual working, but little agreement on the scope of the word "virtual." There is also a vast literature on the various interpretations of "organization." Much depends on the perspective of the writer and the functional training or discipline that the authors have worked in. Indeed, one wit has suggested that the situation regarding virtual organizations is so ambiguous, we need a research project to help us to agree on a definition!

Barnes and Hunt[1] claim that Byrne's[2] definition is "perhaps the most representative:"

"A virtual corporation is a temporary network of independent companies – suppliers, customers, even erstwhile rivals – linked by information technology to share skills, costs, and access to one another's markets. It will have neither central office nor an organization chart. It will have no hierarchy and no vertical integration."

The notion that virtual is synonymous with temporary can be misleading. Plenty of examples of *ad hoc* teams or short-lived alliances can be found, and the flexibility that such partnerships offer is obviously exploited where useful. However, many examples can be found of more permanent arrangements. There is certainly a need to move away from hierarchy and traditional organization charts to partnerships and new business models, but organizations that have absolutely "no" hierarchy or vertical integration are hard to find. The Pentacle Virtual Business School (see Chapter 7) is one of the rare examples.

Virtual and networked organizations are in many instances dependent on technology, but an alternative term – "distributed workforce" – suggests that "going virtual" is not just about technology or telecommunications links. Sales teams operate out of the office; engineers visit sites for installation or repair of telephones, photocopiers and all kinds of other equipment. Such dispersed or distributed workforces are commonplace.

NETWORKS

Let's start with networks. First of all we need to distinguish between physical (computer) networks and networks of people. The latter may include personal networks, business alliances, joint ventures, partnerships, and other similar groupings. To these we must now add wireless communications, which enable very sophisticated networks of mobile workers.

To picture your own organization as a network, think of a hollow globe. Then envision the lines of longitude and latitude around the globe (see Fig. 2.1). At various points, add in nodes to represent your business, your customers, and your suppliers. Now imagine these lines as telecommunication links, the telephone lines that connect your computers and other technological devices. You might prefer the picture of a spider's web, but that is not 3-dimensional. We have worked like this for a long time, but our thinking has been forced into the traditional, hierarchical way of looking at organizational design. The traditional chart emphasized the power and authority structure. The new economy requires a new way of working and a new way of thinking about the way we work.

Thus, networking is certainly not new. Even before the advent of the Internet, we were linked through telephone, fax, and satellite communications. What is happening now is that we have more choice. You will find that terms such as multimedia and information and communication technologies (ICT) are used to cover applications as diverse as e-mail, the Internet, Web-based and wireless communications, as well as workflow, groupware and other specialized business applications. We can choose different business architectures. We can set up partnerships across the globe without the disadvantages of space and time. We can invest in shorter-term joint

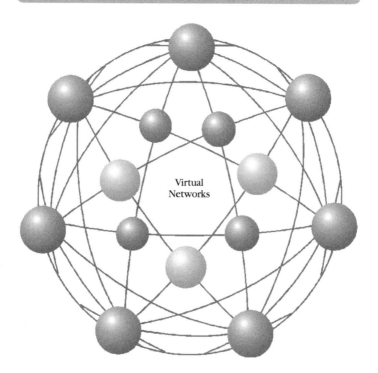

Fig. 2.1 Virtual networks.

ventures and change the configuration of our businesses as frequently as the market demands. The costs of switching and of the technology that makes it possible are so reduced that a new flexibility is possible.

WORKING VIRTUALLY

Davidow and Malone[3] were among the first writers to give us some useful insights into the use of the word "virtual" in a business context. They drew attention to the following:

» *Virtual computers*: In the 1950s, programmers developed machines fast enough to handle several users, whilst each user thought they were the sole user. These "virtual computers" could be used anytime/anyplace. Eventually this led to "virtual reality."

» *Virtual products*: Can mean both physical products and services. They mostly exist in the minds of the teams, in computers, and in flexible production lines. They gave as an example the Japanese "trying in 1992 to 'virtualize' the production of automobiles by putting in place systems that will produce cars to domestic order in just 72 hours."

» *Virtual corporations*: New business structures and architectures with less hierarchy; flatter organizations; fuzzy edges and boundaries. Davidow and Malone did not envision just one form, but saw successful virtual organizations as those who could get to "cost-effective instantaneous production of mass-customized goods and services."

When Davidow and Malone introduced the term "virtual corporation" in 1992 they referred to a broad vision including any new form of organization based on information technology (IT). They had a vision of the corporation of the twenty-first century, and recognized the power that new techniques of information processing would have on the structure of doing business. They saw that time compression was a key business driver in the 1990s, and claimed that the virtual corporation was "now an economic necessity for corporate executives."

The use of the word "virtual" became more common after the introduction of the Internet, a technology that enabled us to link people in many new ways. This particular revolution in telecommunications broke traditional spatial boundaries; allowed us to experiment with new working practices and to set up new business models. The "24 × 7" philosophy challenged our cultural norms, and forced us to re-examine the way we worked.[4]

The idea of an organization as a place has therefore changed: cyberspace[5] must now be included in our definitions. Apart from individuals who work solely on their own, most business organizations must have some territorial assets. However, more and more functions are carried out online that previously needed a branch office, a shop or some physical space. Witness, for instance, the number of bank branches that have closed. Many routine tasks have been automated, and many organizations now route customer contacts through a call center or via Web pages.

Mowshowitz[6] points out that the term "virtual organization" does not presuppose any particular form of organization. He uses the term to denote "the main element in a toolkit for the design of organizations." The notion of *separability* that allows management to switch between different options is important in his definition, as the new flexibility will permit new structures to arise that are tailored to specific needs. He points out that the adjective "virtual" has been applied to a number of activities within the virtual office, the virtual classroom, and the virtual corporation. An important point is that virtual organization can apply to goal-oriented activities[7] – it is not just about structure.

VIRTUAL ORGANIZATIONS: BASIC CONCEPTS

The term "virtual organization" is used to cover a wide range of geographically dispersed organizations, linked by common goals; requiring a new style of management and the reassessment of the role of management; and generally utilizing the Internet and related technologies as a means of communication and collaboration. Interpretation of these concepts must take into account the following.

» *Time and location*: a key element in all thinking about virtual organizations is what is referred to as the "Martini effect" – anytime, anyplace, anywhere. The constraints of time and location are radically reduced.
» *Levels of involvement*:
  » organizational levels of interconnection – whole companies may be working virtually;
  » teams within organizations may be working virtually;
  » individual levels of interconnection and cooperation;
  » general practice: use by the general public, in ways that may or may not impact business practice, such as links to government agencies.

» *Technological advances*: virtual organizations are not synonymous with virtual reality! A number of different technologies are key enablers. Use of information and communication technologies (ICT) has allowed the development of new, flexible ways of working.

In this text:

» we are considering management and behavioral issues rather than technological issues;
» the words virtual and network are often interchangeable; and
» we use the terms virtual and networked organizations to denote networks of people and the use of ICT to restructure organizations and the way people work.

(See Fig. 2.2.)

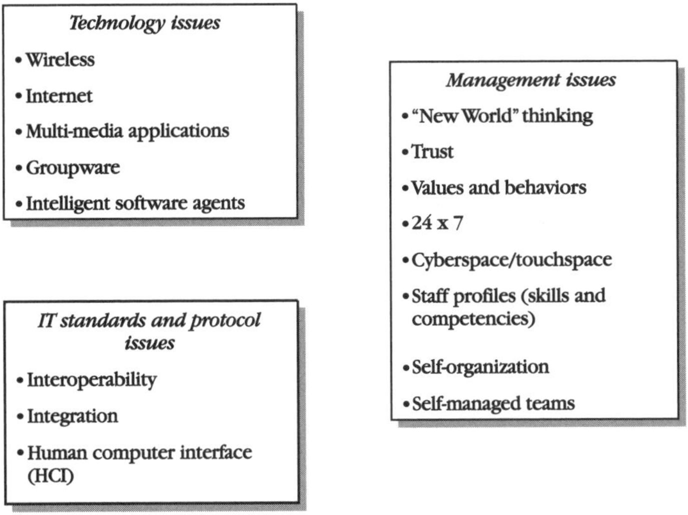

Technology issues

• Wireless
• Internet
• Multi-media applications
• Groupware
• Intelligent software agents

Management issues

• "New World" thinking
• Trust
• Values and behaviors
• 24 x 7
• Cyberspace/touchspace
• Staff profiles (skills and competencies)
• Self-organization
• Self-managed teams

IT standards and protocol issues

• Interoperability
• Integration
• Human computer interface (HCI)

Fig. 2.2   Underpinning concepts and technologies.

NOTES

1 Barnes, S. & Hunt, B. (2001) *E-Commerce & V-Business*. Butterworth-Heinemann.

2 Byrne, J.A. (1993) "The virtual corporation." *Business Week*, February 8, p. 103.

3 Davidow, W. & Malone, M. (1992) *The Virtual Corporation*. Harper-Collins, New York.

4 Martin, J. (1996) *Cybercorp: The New Business Revolution*. AMACOM, New York. www.jamesmartin.com.

5 The term "cyberspace" is often used as a synonym for the Internet. "Cyber" is a prefix to describe a person, thing or idea as part of the computer and information age (for more information see, for example, www.whatis.com).

6 Mowshowitz, A. (1994) "Virtual organization: A vision of management in the information age." *The Information Society*, Vol. 10, pp. 267–88.

7 Mowshowitz, A. (1997) "On the theory of virtual organization." *Syst. Res. Behav. Sci*, Vol. 14, pp. 373–84.

Evolution

We have moved from calculating machines to virtual organizations in 50 years. As change management and people are more important than technology when introducing virtual organizations, this chapter focuses on the changes in management thinking. "Unlearning" traditional ideas and the move to self-organization and knowledge management underpin current developments.

On November 17, 1951 LEO – Lyons Electronic Office – was installed to calculate the value of production at the bakeries of J. Lyons UK. It was the first business system to run on an electronic computer. According to David Caminer,[1] it came about

> "because we wanted something to help to organize even better the many thousands of small transactions that formed the company's business."

In an anniversary article,[2] there is an historic quote from *The Economist* two years later:

> "Opinion is for the moment divided on the place of electronic calculating methods in ordinary business. Is this the first step in an accounting revolution or merely an interesting and expensive experiment?"

From calculating machines to virtual organizations in 50 years!

The study of history is a fascinating hobby, even if we are reluctant to learn from it. There was a time when we talked glibly of "progress" and assumed that mankind was moving forward in an ever-improving cultural continuum, in a fairly straight line. Now our sense of direction is in disarray, and following our path is more like negotiating crazy paving!

We could look at "virtual" by following the evolution of computer applications. If that is your interest, Oravec's book *Virtual Individuals, Virtual Groups*[3] tracks much of the history, with particular reference to Groupware applications. An excellent source for current developments is the *BT Technology Journal*. The Millennium Edition (January 2000) includes a section on the landmarks of telecommunications from 1850 to the present day.

It is argued in this text that new management thinking is needed to cope with current developments. It is therefore appropriate to give a brief overview of evolution from a business point of view. Two themes are intertwined: theories of management and their impact on organizational design.

TWENTIETH CENTURY MANAGEMENT THOUGHT

Working virtually involves redesigning work: an organization should be designed to allow the work to get done. Does form follow function in your organization? Or is it still dominated by a formal, hierarchical power structure? The stifling influence of the bureaucratic model is a serious constraint in today's dynamic business world. It is concerned with the organization chart, division of labor, spans of control, and scalar relationships (the chain of command). It divides work into functions and each department builds walls to protect itself. These "stove pipes" constrain the flow of work which, to be effective, must be studied as process flows.

Management thinking in the early twentieth century was dominated by a series of ideas that are still influential today.

» The *classical* movement, which is associated with the scientific management ideas of Taylor, Gilbreth, and Gantt and Fayol.
» The *behavioral* approach, which led to the human relations movement and recognition of a people-orientated approach to management.
» The *management science* approach, which emphasized quantitative methods.
» *Contingency theory*, which suggests that everything managers do has to be related to specific circumstances, and directly contradicts the "one best way" of scientific management thinking.
» *Systems thinking*, which was a reaction against the reductionism of scientific management and introduced a holistic perspective into management.

In 1986 Gareth Morgan[4] presented a fascinating overview of interpretations of organizations. It was not just a history of organization theory. It challenged conventional ways of examining organizations. Another interesting survey was presented by Strage,[5] who concluded that:

> "The art/science/practice of management has developed, as this eclectic collection shows, unevenly over time and by nationality ... there is no easily discernible logic or sequence to the development of the ideas and concepts described."

He states that as he cannot find any consistent pattern, such as is found in branches of science such as physics,

> "perhaps management is not a science after all, even though some of us in the 1950s and later tried to persuade ourselves that it was."

The tendency to think in terms of the past is reflected in many textbooks. In 1994 Wren[6] still does not include "virtual" in his index, and suggests just four main periods of evolution including the nineteenth century pioneers:

1 Early management thought:
   » management problems arising in early factories
   » early pioneers such as Owen.
2 The scientific management era:
   » Taylor and efficiency models
   » the emergence of human factors
   » management and organization theories
   » Fayol and Weber.
3 The social person era:
   » the Hawthorne studies
   » the search for organizational integration
   » Follett and Barnard
   » changing assumptions about people at work.
4 The modern era:
   » renaissance of general management
   » organizational behavior and theory
   » science and systems in management.

A recent distance learning book[7] devotes a chapter to the relationships between employees and management. Traditional topics are included:

» coordination, organizational structure and design;
» job design and work structuring;
» design of hierarchies;
» centralization and decentralization; and
» bureaucratic and organic structures.

At the very end of the chapter, there is just a half page on ''the virtual firm!'' This is described as ''an extreme example of an alliance'' and ''at the opposite extreme from the sort of business most of us work for.''

However, by the end of the twentieth century, management thinking had begun to take account of the introduction of business systems and the growth of the Internet.

» *The learning organization* was a recognition of the need to proactively create, share, and transfer information.
» *Knowledge management* became a formal way of encouraging innovation and lifelong learning.

Bruce Mazlish[8] expressed a far more radical point of view. He first of all discussed the three ''discontinuities'' suggested by Freud – the three great thinkers who had ''outraged man's naïve self-love'' – Copernicus, Darwin, and Freud himself. Mazlish then states that the human ego is undergoing another shock:

> ''To put it bluntly, we are now coming to realize that humans and the machines they create are continuous and that the same conceptual schemes that help explain the workings of the brain also explain the workings of a 'thinking machine'.''

His thesis is that humans are on the point of:

> ''breaking past the discontinuity between themselves and machines.''

As we investigate the extent to which we are working virtually, this last point becomes increasingly valid.

LANDMARKS

Study of business practices demonstrates that there has been a continuum, and virtual organizations are part of that evolution. On the way, we have experimented with many well-intentioned but uncoordinated initiatives. Technological developments have been steadily speeding up the rate of change, so that we have moved from an "if it ain't broke, don't fix it" mentality, through continuous improvement and incremental change, to radical step changes.

Evolution has been closely linked to developments in manufacturing. Pearson[9] suggested *Seven Ages of Factory Man*:

» Fordian man;
» automation man;
» low inventory man;
» balanced man;
» integrated man;
» low overhead man; and
» quality man.

To which he then added:

» flexible man;
» service man; and
» enterprise man.

To these we can now add another:

» virtual man.

Key episodes in the evolution of world class manufacturing included the move from *Total Quality Control* (TQC) in the 1970s, through *Total Quality Management* (TQM) in the 1980s, to *World Class Manufacturing* in the 1990s. In the last decade, managers began to recognize the need to extend these changes across the whole business. The application of systems thinking began to show results as managers recognized processes and interdependencies. These first moves away from functional thinking were seen in *Computer Integrated Manufacturing* (CIM), later followed by *Enterprise Resource Planning* (ERP).

The use of the *Internet* as a business tool (rather than for military use) saw the beginning of what Malone and Laubacher[10] call the "e-lance" economy. They claimed that by "changing the way work is done, electronic networks may lead to a new kind of economy centered on the individual." They foresaw the growth of temporary companies and "elastic" networks.

Manugistics[11] provide an excellent summary of the evolution of businesses in their "Compass" diagram (Fig. 3.1).

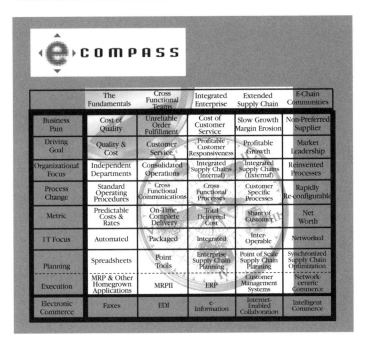

Fig. 3.1 Compass diagram. (Courtesy of Sam Brown, Manugistics.)

Study of evolutionary trends indicates a move from functional approaches to management and organization to a focus on:

» customer interactions;
» purchasing and logistics; and
» knowledge management/information processing.

The idea of organization as synonymous with place is thus challenged. The emphasis is moving away from the task and power structures depicted in traditional charts of management hierarchy. Processes become key. The new model demands not only a rethink of functional divisions, but also of the implications of the application of technology and the impact of the changes on employees. The human aspects of the change to computer-integrated management as the basis of new business models are extensive. Resource development, new skill profiles, organizational design, job retraining, elimination of redundant activities, together with the many aspects of human–computer interfaces, all become key factors.

This is well illustrated by the growth of *teleworking*. Although the term was originally applied to people working at home, it covers a wide range of activities carried out remotely. Qvortrup[12] lists several terms such as flexi-workers, satellite office workers and distance workers, and points out that the words are not synonymous. They cover different technical, geographical, organizational and legal criteria.

Virtual organizations dissolve space, time, and organizational boundaries, using new technologies to enable new ways of working and new potential business models. The idea of an integrated business, breaking down functional barriers and managing a business as a series of processes, was enabled by several software developments. *Business Process Re-engineering* (BPR) was an important driver of such changes in nonmanufacturing functions. The move from aggressive, price-driven purchasing to single-source supply drove the revolution in supply chain management. Once business relationships became long-term, it was worthwhile investing in standardized computer systems. Where systems are still incompatible, much work is needed on connectivity, interoperability, standards, and protocols. This applied as much to the ''old'' technologies such as EDI as to the new Web-based interfaces.

The introduction of *concurrent engineering* and the use of *cross-functional teams* in research and design were an early form of networking. By cooperating with all those who contributed to the final product or service, time and cost could be taken out of the system, and engineering changes could be minimized. These techniques have now been applied to all parts of our organizations. *Self-managed, high performance teams* in all parts of the organization have developed from these experiments in concurrent engineering. Many new software applications were initially internal systems, to provide the ability to interact with a common corporate database for a comprehensive range of applications. Using Web interfaces, these now provide e-business, *relationship management* and supply chain management applications: the basis of the virtual enterprise. In fact, from integration it could be said we have moved to "disintegration!"

COMPANIES: WHAT ARE THEY?[13]

The UK Royal Society for Arts, Manufactures and Commerce (RSA) led a major study into the future of organizations – *Tomorrow's Company*.[14] Presenting the findings in June 1995, the inquiry chairman, Sir Anthony Cleaver, described them as "practical, specific and relevant to the current business scene."[15] In his commentary, Mark Goyder, the program director, pointed out that:

> "The inclusive company advocated by the RSA Inquiry is a deceptively obvious concept. Most of its elements can be expressed in terms of received wisdom. 'Your people are your greatest asset.' 'Know your strengths.' 'Let everyone know where you stand.' 'Build trust, never stop learning.'"

With the escalation of virtual working, it will be even harder to implement such concepts. As the boundaries of organizations are increasingly fluid, managing the disparate elements is harder than ever before. As technology can now be used to monitor and control both people and processes, it could be argued that not only has the role of the manager changed: managers as we have known them are obsolete. Confirmation of this change is found in the growth of:

» self-management and self-organization;
» teleworking; and
» the notion that we do not have careers, but a "portfolio of activities."

Individuals demonstrate their preferences by their attention to quality of working life issues, and by adopting virtual working. A fundamental shift is taking place.

FIT FOR THE FUTURE?

Managing the future has become a common theme in management texts. Phrases such as "rethinking the enterprise" or "creating new futures'' are almost clichés. As Micklethwait and Wooldridge[16] point out:

> "even the best managers have found that fine-tuning traditional command-and-control systems is subject to the law of diminishing returns."

There was a time when we taught employees to "institutionalize change!" Now we demand that they unlearn what they were taught and continually reinvent themselves as well as their organizations.

It may be more useful to look for advice on how to survive in the future, than to look at the past. Fielder[17] provides us with some useful guidelines. He claims that we ignore these trends at our peril.

» "Bend me, shape me:" A move to self-employment and a portfolio of activities.
» "Internal dialogue:" Initiatives such as 360° appraisal will be an important part of cultural change within organizations.
» "Knowledge management:" Internal knowledge is being counted as an asset. This internal "memory bank" is key to innovation.
» "Managing messaging:" In a world of increasing information overload, we have to learn to manage the deluge of messages that arrive every day.
» "Customer focusing:" The hard-hitting aggressive tactics of yesteryear are no longer tolerated.
» "*Parlez-vous* foreign?:" In spite of increasing globalization, many people, especially in the UK, are slow to learn other languages.
» "Develop your feminine side:" Adjusting to the new culture means more attention must be paid to the "soft" side of business relationships.
» "Find time (and manage stress):" As more business is 24 × 7, there will be even more pressure on employees who are trying to balance work and home life.
» "Own new technology:" Unless you are computer-literate (but not necessarily a programmer), you will find it hard to compete.
» "Vocation transformation:"[18] Align your personal aspirations with the work you do.

ECONOMIC AND ORGANIZATIONAL EVOLUTION

See Table 3.1[19]

Table 3.1   Economic and organizational evolution. (Source: Miles, R. et al., 2000.)

Economic era	Standardization	Customization	Innovation
Meta-capability	Coordination	Delegation	Collaboration
Business model	Market penetration	Market segmentation	Market exploration
Growth driver	Learning curve gains and scale	Know-how transfer	Entrepreneurial empowerment
Organizational model	Functional	Divisional matrix and network	Alliances, spin-offs, federations
Key asset	Tangible assets	Information	Knowledge

NOTES

1 Caminer's article can be downloaded from www.comjnl.oupjournals.org. (1997) *Browse the Archive*, Vol 40, No 10.
2 "How Leo Started It All." *The Computer Bulletin*, November 2001, pp. 26-27.
3 Oravec, J. (1996) *Virtual Individuals, Virtual Groups*. Cambridge University Press, Cambridge.
4 Morgan, G. (1986) *Images of Organization*. Sage.
5 Strage, H. (ed.) (1992) *Milestones in Management*. Blackwell, Oxford.
6 Wren, D.A. (1994) *The Evolution of Management Thought*. John Wiley.
7 (2000) *Management Principles*. BPP.
8 Mazlish, B. (1993) *The Fourth Discontinuity*. Yale University Press.
9 Pearson, D. (1991) "The seven ages of factory man." *Director*. October, pp. 118-19. NB: no sexism is implied in this list!
10 Malone, T. & Laubacher, R. (1998) "The Dawn of the e-lance Economy." *HBR*, September, pp. 145-52.
11 Thanks to Sam Brown at Manugistics www.manugistics.com.

12 Qvortup, L. (1998) in *Teleworking: International Perspectives* (ed. Jackson, P. & Van der Wielen, J.). Routledge.

13 De Geus, A. (1995) "Companies: what are they?" Lecture delivered to the RSA, printed in June 1995 issue of the *RSA Journal.*

14 RSA, 8 John Adam Street, London WC2N 6EZ, UK. Note also Goyder, M. (1998) *Living Tomorrow's Company*. Gower.

15 Reported in RSA Journal, August (1995).

16 Micklethwait, J. & Wooldridge, A. (1996) *The Witch Doctors.* Mandarin.

17 Fielder, D. (2000) "Fit for the future?" *Informatics*, January, pp. 10-12.

18 Williams, N. (1999) *The Work We Were Born To Do*. Element.

19 From Miles, R. et al. (2000) "The future.org." *Long Range Planning*, Vol. 33 (3), pp. 300-321.

The E-Dimension

The scope of virtual organizations is so vast, this chapter concentrates on disintermediation: the removal of the middleman and the move to a self-service model. These changes are illustrated by case studies.

» The financial sector – stockbroking as entertainment!
» Online recruitment and appraisal systems.
» The virtual university.

The mind-map in Fig. 4.1 shows the extraordinary scope of the ''e-dimension.'' The suggested categories help us to cope with the vast variety involved. A common factor is the use of the Internet as a tool for communications and collaboration. Another is the move to self-service models.

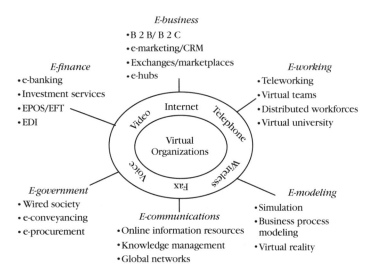

Fig. 4.1 The scope of virtual and networked organizations.

DISINTERMEDIATION

A key feature of the e-business story is the growth of self-service models. These eliminate the ''middle man'' and reliance on third parties, and are referred to as ''disintermediation.'' For example, in the finance sector, banks are closing local branches; passengers are increasingly booking flights on the Internet rather than using a travel agent. Online auctions such as www.eBay.com provide the means of exchanging goods without leaving home. Users can gain direct access to information or services, usually using the Internet as the communications medium. The revolutionary changes that are taking place can be illustrated by redrawing our organizational charts. Figure 4.2, the Origo[1] "Roadmap," is a vivid demonstration of current changes.

Although this is an example from the financial sector, it can be applied to many situations. The service provider used to contact clients via a broker or agent (illustrated by the center line). Numerous software applications have been developed to provide efficiency and productivity gains, but clients now have a choice of media through which to contact the service provider directly. These include the Internet, wireless technology and digital TV.

Here, for reasons of space, we are illustrating disintermediation with just three case studies:

» changes in the financial services – a personal account from Justin Urquart Stewart;
» the increasing impact of the Internet on human resources management; and
» the virtual university and the move to e-learning.

Further examples of disintermediation – e-stores and e-banking – are illustrated in Chapter 7. Call centers are an important facet of our self-service society. Analysis of their progress reflects the growth of virtual and networked organizations. There is insufficient space to give call centers the attention they deserve – see Collins (2001)[2] for a report on current developments.

STOCKBROKING AS ENTERTAINMENT?

Justin Urquart Stewart,[3] a well-known writer on financial matters, suggests that we need to totally reassess our attitude to all types of business. Using stockbroking as an example, he points out that trying to keep up with the changes in the investment community and the different types of investors is increasingly difficult. Until a few years ago stockbrokers looked after their clients in a delightfully old-fashioned way. The idea that people could manage, trade, and find out information about their shares had not occurred to them at all. They had to learn a new way of working. The new era means that you have to get used to the idea that business is not something that is just 9–5; it is not

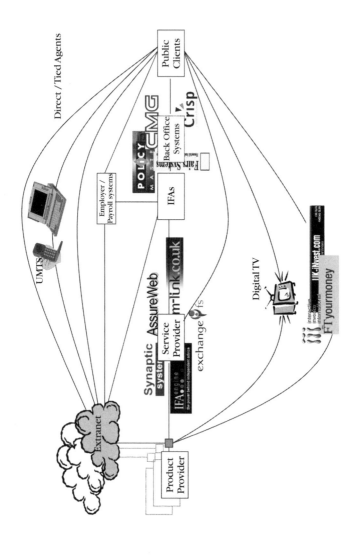

Fig. 4.2 The Origo environment. (© Origo Systems Ltd 2001.)

a standard product and service; it is not just a commoditized facility. You are trying to turn it into something that has relevance to your customers. If it is not relevant, people will leave because there is always somebody willing to do it more cheaply, in a different way, or even free.

Customer focus is a rather apple-pie-and-motherhood phrase, but it does mean that you have to be more proactive. When you go through a dealing process with a client, you realize that as a broker you have a lot of experience in all the different products that people put together throughout the world. Then you realize that many clients have no idea what you are talking about.

Other groups of clients will not just question you; they may be ahead of you. And they may be right, even though you hope you are better informed than they are. The traditional structure of the advisor's relationship has changed radically. Stockbroking is becoming a very important hobby – part of the entertainment business. Urquart Stewart thinks that the stockmarket is a bit like a soap opera. Every day there is a different story and someone is nervous about it because something has gone hideously wrong. It is a story and even better than a soap opera as people can and do get involved in it. Every one of us has a connection, even if only through our pension schemes.

A different approach to business is therefore essential. How do you react to all this change? You have to ask yourself some difficult questions.

» Is your work a hobby?
» What sort of business do you think you are in now?
» Are you any better than anyone else?
» Why is anyone going to stay with you?

KEY ISSUES IN THE FINANCIAL SECTOR

» Real-time share trading.
» Security.
» Transparency – fund managers are exposed to an educated audience for the first time.

- » System design to combine both the customer and the provider needs.
- » Flexible systems and flexible attitudes to your customer needs.
- » Staff adaptability.
- » Design for redundancy – plan for continuous changes in demand levels, products, volumes, and technology.
- » Government and international regulations will impact the way you do business.
- » Self-service.
- » Multimedia access – according to customer needs.
- » Product differentiation.

ONLINE RECRUITMENT

An interesting aspect of virtual working can be illustrated by investigating the application of technology within the human resources department. Automating the more obvious administrative tasks such as expenses claims and changes to personnel records can save time and money, and hugely improve operational productivity around the world. Other aspects have wider implications.

The nature of recruitment has entirely changed: the whole world becomes your catchment area, so organizations can choose between two options:

- » recruiting advertisements on their own Website; or
- » online recruitment agencies.

The online recruitment industry in Europe is set to rise from £50mn in 1999 to £3.8bn by 2005, according to Taylor.[4] There are already 300 online recruitment providers in the UK and 1400 across Europe. Their main job is to hold and display a big database of CVs and to post job advertisements on the Internet. Some other services that online agencies may provide are HR software, candidate tracking tools, and online interviewing facilities.

Peter Cappelli[5] points out that by making it easy for people to submit applications, companies have also to have procedures to sort these applications quickly without screening out the good candidates. In companies that use their own Website for recruiting, this sorting can be done automatically. Key questions can be used to screen out inappropriate candidates. In addition, there are some Internet-based systems of tracking and selecting candidates. These systems (HMS – hiring management systems) are used by big companies, but more often by recruiting agencies. More specifically, these systems can collect applications in standardized form, screen them, determine where they came from (recruitment agencies or classified advertisements), monitor the applications, and calculate how long it takes to fill the various vacancies. In the USA, only 10% of large companies use this kind of system, but this percentage is increasing.

Hauenstein[6] states that there is an increase in the use of interview guides. Russell[7] quotes the use of online questionnaires using 40 multiple-choice and several open-ended questions. During the first five months of one system's operation there were 6000 job applicants, of whom about 40% were eliminated automatically by the "machine."

The aims of using online methods include lower recruiting costs, a faster recruiting cycle, and the choice of higher caliber recruits. There are claims that Internet recruitment can reduce the cost per recruit by 80% compared to newspaper advertisements. It may be that this method also finds a better quality of candidate because Internet users tend to be better-educated and more computer literate than nonusers. However, as Cappelli stated, "if it's much easier for a company to hire experienced workers, it's also much easier for competitors to hire away a company's personnel." Cappelli is also concerned about discrimination and data protection, as laws vary according to the country in which you are doing business.

Eventually, there will probably be an entirely different scenario. When organizations get used to this new method of recruiting, they may reverse the traditional view of recruitment. They could well use intelligent software agents to trawl the Net looking for candidates, rather than wait for applicants to find them. Jobseekers are already leaving their CVs online for potential employers to find. Some companies, such as British Airways, now only receive applications from graduates through Websites. For big companies that face skill shortages, online recruitment may be the best way to fill vacancies. In a very competitive and global environment, the Web can help them to find suitable people from all around the world.

ONLINE APPRAISAL SYSTEMS

When your employees are spread around the world, it is tempting to simplify as many functions as possible by using automated systems. Personnel specialists will tell you that any interactions with high emotional content require a 1:1 meeting. Appraisals are usually included within this category. However, companies such as Royal Dutch Shell already use online systems for 360° appraisal, and these are far more controversial than many other online applications.

An interesting debate on the issue of online psychometric testing was published in *People Management*.[8] Robert McHenry is cynical about Internet-based assessment. He writes that consumers do want simple, more efficient, and cheaper systems, but believes that the trend is being:

> "push-started by accountants and entrepreneurs promising clients a 10-minute wonder-test that will spot the duds among their applicants at a fraction of the usual cost."

However, as testing is a human interaction, McHenry believes that:

> "if you take this element away you'll soon lose the real customers: the candidates themselves."

In the same feature, Russell Drakeley suggests that the threat to standards is too great to be acceptable:

> "Search for 'personality tests' on the Internet and see what rubbish you will turn up. It hardly enhances the reputation of our industry."

In contrast, Richard Alberg is in favor of online assessment, and says that:

"Results are held on a central server, which will significantly improve the predictive quality of tests, as publishers become able to analyse vast quantities of data."

The potential of such systems is a key area of research but it will be some time before definitive answers can be given.

THE VIRTUAL UNIVERSITY

"Education over the Internet is going to be so big it is going to make e-mail usage look like a rounding error in terms of the Internet capacity it will consume."

John Chambers (Cisco)

"The user needs to accept that this is a different way of learning, and learn to deal with the differences. This is, after all, as it ought to be. There is no point simply reproducing on the web what can be done in a book."

Uschi Felix[9]

Internet-based learning is becoming an important social instrument as well as a tool for companies that wish to extend their training programs. The center of debate is the growth of "e-learning" or the "virtual university." For many years, academics have been using various software applications to aid their teaching, from basic word-processing, databases, spreadsheets to e-mail, Web-based resources, and other Internet sources. Now their challenge is to compete with the increasing number of organizations offering online learning "packages."

It is useful to compare universities to businesses, and to ask the same business questions:

» What business are we in? What are we trying to be?
» What is the purpose of education? What are the current expectations of education systems?
» What is the nature of the (educational) supply chain? Do you regard your students as "customers" or "products?"

» What partnerships or formal links are required?
» Does an institution want to be one of the elite? Or in the middle range, providing no-nonsense, good-quality education? Or should it be positioned as a "fast-food" outlet, providing a basic but limited set of options?

The drivers behind change include:

» focus on the knowledge economy;
» an enriched educational environment that encourages lifelong learning;
» demand for greater productivity;
» the potential of information technology to enhance the learning experience; and
» the potential of information technology to reach out to groups of people previously excluded from access.

It is estimated that by 2002, 84% of colleges and universities will offer distance-learning courses in some form. It is now more useful to talk about "distributed" learning rather than "distance" learning, as the technology makes the learning local to the user (see Fig. 4.3).

Heriot-Watt University (Scotland) developed this model. They use a relatively low-tech solution, and provide local support for learners in approved support centers (ASCs) around the world. The principles underlying this model are:

» student-centered learning;
» self-paced;
» face-to-face tutorial support from local partners;
» team working;
» skill development;
» strong subject emphasis.

An increasing number of companies are providing their own "virtual university." The Cisco case study is an interesting one.[10] Not only has the company adopted a policy of actively encouraging its partners and customers to use the Web; it is aiding the process by spending time to help anyone who uses traditional methods to learn how to use the Web. Thus, frequently asked questions (FAQs) are all on the Web, so

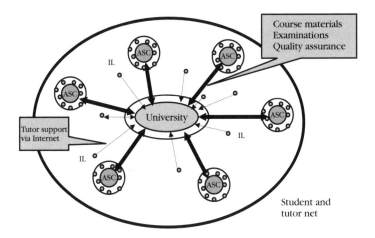

Fig. 4.3 Distributed campus.

that internal and external people can use a self-service approach. More than that, Cisco use online training, and set up a "Career Certifications" program. In November 1999, they announced an e-learning initiative, a move that meant that the company would "shift its entire training structure to an e-learning model." One of the drivers cited was that e-learning makes students more accountable, through online testing and progress management. Virtual Lab Technology provides a 24×7 live network "solely dedicated to the rapid acquisition and reinforcement of IT skills." It is important here to note that training online is rather different to education online. To make all learning mechanistic and akin to rote learning would certainly not produce the creativity and innovation that businesses require.

The new education model requires students (that term refers to people of all ages and in all walks of life) to take responsibility for their own learning. We need to move from the "sage on the stage" to the "guide on the side." A critical success factor, as in all situations, is to have a well-thought-out strategy and implementation plan. If there is just a jumble of projects with no overriding scheme to provide a logical framework and progression, e-learning will neither inspire nor develop. To quote Marc Rosenberg:[11]

"The question is no longer whether organizations will implement online learning, but whether they will do it well."

A SPECIAL CASE: VIRTUAL LANGUAGE LEARNING

Professor Uschi Felix from Monash University, Australia, has researched this topic extensively. She has produced a book that includes a CD-ROM containing references to Websites providing aids to teachers. This allows instant cross-referencing. Professor Felix recognizes the attractions of the Web, and points out that there are many public resources that do not require permission to access. She suggests that for students, the Web offers:

» experience beyond the confines of the curriculum;
» authentic experiences of the target culture;
» flexibility of time and place;
» constant access to materials; and
» chat rooms (with teachers or other students).

Realistically, there will be some drawbacks:

» slow modem connections;
» a computer that is not state-of-the-art so that plug-ins etc. are hard to handle;
» slow response rates;
» lack of user-friendliness on Websites;
» volatility of sites – they may be restructured or disappear; and
» protected sites where a fee is payable.

Professor Felix suggests that many resources are created for a specific purpose or environment – "materials are not neatly structured as they are in a familiar textbook, and the larger the resource, the more complex the links to other relevant sites, the greater the chance of ending up somewhere completely unexpected." The latter is part of the fun of the Web, but for the uninitiated, it can be daunting.

She gives examples of French, Spanish, Italian, German, and Scandinavian languages, and discusses the problems of languages such as Thai that require different character fonts. Chinese, Japanese, and Korean pose particular problems for computers with a set of only 256 characters (basic Japanese has over 6000 characters, for example).

Only experimentation will bring home how easy this is. It is fascinating to log on and listen to another language being spoken. It is also fun to try out the interactive activities. Try some of the sites listed in Chapter 9.

NOTES

1 Courtesy Origo Services Ltd: www.origoservices.com.

2 Collins, P. (ed.) (2001) "From call centre to multimedia customer interaction centre," Conference Proceedings, Access Conferences Ltd., Dublin.

3 Justin Urquart Stewart: www.7im.co.uk. See Collins, P. (ed.) (2001) "From call centre to multimedia customer interaction centre," Conference Proceedings, Access Conferences Ltd., Dublin.

4 Taylor, C. (2001) "Windows of opportunity." *People Management*, March 8, pp. 32–36.

5 Capelli, P. (2001) "Making the most of online recruiting." *Harvard Business Review*, March, pp. 139–46 and www.hbr.org.

6 Hauenstein, P. (2000) "The impact of the Internet on the hiring interview." www.advantagehiring.com/newsletter.

7 Russell, J. "Hiring the electronic way." www.informationweek.com.

8 (2001) *People Management*, June 14, pp. 26–37.

9 Uschi Felix, http://www-personal.monash.edu.au/~ufelix/index.htm

10 www.cisco.com.

11 Rosenberg, M. (2001) *E-Learning: Strategies For Delivering Knowledge In The Digital Age*. McGraw-Hill, New York.

The Global Dimension

The global village depends on the Internet and other communications technologies. Supply networks are increasingly sophisticated and the network has replaced the chain metaphor. We now have to incorporate new e-business models:

» e-procurement
» marketplaces and exchanges
» e-hubs.

''Companies expect 78% of their customers and 65% of their trading partners to have global electronic connections with them by 2002. Also, the Internet continues to spawn new market models around bids, auctions, and exchanges. The result: a continuous influx of new players with which to share processes and technologies.''

Forrester Research

''The company that delivers the same high level of service regardless of interaction method has a distinct market advantage.''

Aberdeen Group

THE GLOBAL VILLAGE

Marshall McLuhan coined the term ''the global village'' in the 1960s. He believed that the world would be completely changed by the use of telecommunications. The political, economic, and social implications of globalization – whether or not it is the ''Americanization'' of the world; the costs and benefits of free trade; or the environmental and cultural impacts it brings about – are vitally important issues.[1]

According to Michael Porter,[2] in the global economy ''much of the conventional wisdom about how companies and nations compete needs to be overhauled.'' Porter's contribution to the debate centers on what he terms ''clusters'' – ''geographic concentrations of interconnected companies and institutions in a particular field.'' A particularly interesting observation is that

''Competition can coexist with cooperation because they occur on different dimensions and among different players ... Clusters represent a kind of new spatial organization.''

In this chapter we are going to look at supply networks, a good example of new spatial organization. Cyberspace has been described as the ''total interconnectedness of human beings through computers and telecommunications, without regard to physical geography.''[3] The use of the Internet and related technologies has enabled organizations to experiment with new global models. Conventional wisdom is being overhauled on more than one plane. Trading on the Web is about redefining your business model, and accepting that there are different rules for B2B (business to business) and for B2C (business to consumer); but you forget fundamental business rules at your peril. There is a new agenda:

> "Business agility and the ability to grow revenue and profit at the same time, is the new mandate for business and IT executives."[4]

It is a constantly evolving scenario. Nicky Kibble of IBM suggests that the evolution of e-business has gone through several phases, from e-procurement to e-logistics to the e-enterprise. She links this with the development of knowledge management and business intelligence gathering.

The failure of the dotcoms caused a major panic and many people thought that it meant the end of e-business. Wrong! It did mean that at last people realized that having fantastic technology is not enough. You need a business case and a business strategy whatever the means by which you choose to operate. Developments were greatly hindered by the hype and overinvestment in fragile dotcoms. There was far too much incompetent management in the early days. Fulfillment was severely neglected in the rush to develop attractive Web pages.

The Internet reduces the entry barriers for newcomers and eliminates intermediaries. Customers have access to so much information, even if they do not buy on the Web they are increasingly better informed. If their expectations are not met, they are far more likely to switch to another supplier who is now only a click away. Switching costs are drastically reduced and the customer has far more bargaining power. In addition, it has become clear that a simple site cannot provide the fast access now expected – browsers have access to millions of documents in many different formats – so scalability to cope with the volume of business is crucial. If it takes more than 8 seconds to download, 50% of browsers will move onto another Website. The ability to personalize your site for individual customers is also important in the fight to retain customers.

Interviewed by Joan Margretta,[5] Michael Dell concluded that:

> "The direct system really delivers value to the customer all the way from distribution back through manufacturing and design. If you

tried to divide Dell up into a manufacturer and a channel, you'd destroy the company's unique value. It's something completely new that nobody in our industry has ever done before."

Dell began their new system in 1984. Now even giants such as IBM are adopting the model. People, processes, strategy, and technology all underpin the dynamics of the supply chain. Time and time again, directors, managers, and consultants alike stress this point. You need what Mark Barratt[6] refers to as an "e-business toolkit:" you need to subdivide your operations into e-procurement, marketplaces (also known as exchanges), e-auctions, and e-fulfillment; you add in a collaborative planning process, and call in the assistance of companies that know how to implement enterprise-wide integrated applications. Barratt lists critical issues and success factors including:

» industry knowledge
» partnerships
» technology
» service offering versus speed
» standards
» connection to other marketplaces
» content management
» integration.

SUPPLY CHAIN NETWORKS

The road to creating intelligent e-business networks started with the humble fax machine. Through e-mail, EDI, and extranets the route has now reached a state referred to as "intelligent commerce" – a form of trading making increasing use of intelligent software agents. The aim is to improve planning and decision-making across all the key business processes – a very much more sophisticated version of business process re-engineering than that envisioned in the early phases of that concept in the 1990s.

Sam Brown from Manugistics[7] has suggested that the network has now replaced the chain as the supply metaphor (Fig. 5.1).

Brown also suggests that the key issues in current performance are:

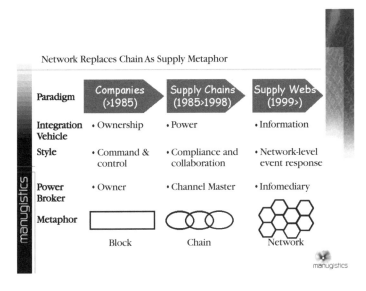

Fig. 5.1 Network replaces chain as supply metaphor.

» information delays and distortion between levels in the supply chain (e.g. leading to parts shortages);
» planning activities are not synchronized and closed loop (resulting in long lead times);
» high levels of forecast variability (leading to low percentage of on-time shipments and frequent expediting);
» lack of visibility to exception conditions; and
» no inter-enterprise process optimization.

The complexity of today's markets is leading to:

» increased outsourcing;
» companies returning to core competencies;
» reduction of working capital;
» increased velocity of orders and information;
» disparate demand signals across multiple channels;

» participation in private and public trading exchanges;
» globalization;
» rapid expansion of overseas operations;
» increased global sourcing amongst vendors; and
» dynamic and complex trading communities.

According to Evans and Wurster,[8] the second generation of electronic commerce will be shaped more by strategy than by experimentation. The battle for competitive advantage will be waged along three dimensions: reach, affiliation, and richness. Reach is about access and connection; richness is the depth and detail of information the business makes available for the customer; and affiliation means that you have to think about your customers in a completely different way. When you contact your customers via the Web, the interface and the help that you offer can be your competitive advantage. Those firms that only automate current practices will be overtaken by those that manage collaborative partnerships. The impact of poor supply chain management is loss of market value.

E-PROCUREMENT IN THE OIL AND GAS INDUSTRY

Laura McKee at Bywater[9] has provided some very interesting statistics on e-procurement. They have produced this graph of e-procurement expenditure that helps to keep the size of this sector in perspective (Fig. 5.2).

They state that research into expected savings from e-procurement range from 12% to 34%. Taking one sector, oil and gas, they show the relationship between different types of approaches and the new methods available (Table 5.1).

Bywater state that most of the operators who have implemented e-procurement strategies have taken a two-phase approach:

1 Drive buy-price savings through the use of e-auction and volume for margin;
2 Achieve process savings and total cost of ownership reductions through evaluating the total procurement cycle.

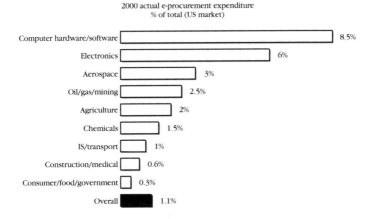

2000 actual e-procurement expenditure
% of total (US market)

Computer hardware/software — 8.5%
Electronics — 6%
Aerospace — 3%
Oil/gas/mining — 2.5%
Agriculture — 2%
Chemicals — 1.5%
IS/transport — 1%
Construction/medical — 0.6%
Consumer/food/government — 0.3%
Overall — 1.1%

Fig. 5.2   Percentage of industry procurement which is electronic.

Table 5.1   Oil and gas procurement categories.

Category	Description	Examples	Current approaches
Strategies	Low volume, high value, core products	Rigs 4D seismic topside equipment Complex well solutions Major capital items	E-enabled supply chain integration
Operational	Routine expenditure for core operations	Scaffolding Well equipment Maintenance Down hole solutions Service contract	No clear approach
Commodity	High volume, low value items	Spares Non-critical operating items Basic chemicals	Catalogue Auction Outsource

To date, they have found that in this sector:

> "The challenge of technology, adoption, standards, and sustainability are preventing the benefits from being realized throughout the value chain."

MARKETPLACES AND EXCHANGES

In 2000, we were trying to find a way to make our Internet strategies look and sound better than those of our competitors. B2C and B2B were the catch phrases we all had to learn. By 2001 along came exchanges and we had to readjust yet again. There are plenty of illustrations of this phenomenon. Yet again Cisco is a role model, but Carrefour is also an interesting case to follow. Covisint is the auto trade exchange.[10] There are fears in some quarters that these agreements could become monopolies. However, the volume of trade between partners is so great that any model that can both reduce administrative costs and handling/data entry errors is seen as a huge benefit to industry.

The Internet changed the nature of supply chain management; linear inventory flows have been replaced by multidirectional flows; and life is further complicated by online auctions and other mechanisms. As business partners are now dispersed all over the globe, and forecasting even less reliable in the fragmented trading networks of today, the growth of marketplaces and exchanges is not surprising. Sam Brown distinguishes three major types of exchange.

Enterprise networks
» One to many.
» Extending supply chains suppliers and customers.
» Focused on the dominating player.
» Savvy way to leverage the extended supply chain.

Vertical e-marketplaces
» One to many or many to many.
» Enables collaboration between various players in an industry.
» Gives access to a wider audience.

Horizontal e-marketplaces

» Many to many.
» Access to specific functionality such as transport or excess auctioning.

He predicts that the B2B revolution will mean that business trading networks of the future will incorporate exchange frameworks, procurement and sourcing, logistics brokering, and overall trading network optimization.

CASE STUDY: CISCO'S eHUB INITIATIVE

Brown describes the eHub vision as "enabling seamless integration of inter-enterprise supply chain planning and execution processes," together with the added benefits of better demand forecasting.

Grosvenor and Austin[11] have published a valuable case study on Cisco's eHub initiative. These authors suggest that many companies tend to adopt a wait-and-see policy as they cannot see where the volatile markets are heading. Cisco considers such a strategy as deadly. They launched eHub – a move from point-to-point to "a hub-and-spoke model of information flow and collaboration" – in 2001. This launch followed a pilot with Motorola in the previous year. eHub is a private trading e-marketplace that embraces at least 2000 of their supply chain partners. The vision is "to keep Cisco and its manufacturing trading partners on the leading edge of e-business technology adoption."

According to Grosvenor and Austin, the following lessons were among those learned from this project.

» Executive sponsorship is an essential foundation.
» Shared vision and a passion to achieve it are necessary.
» Open communication and collaboration are the lifeblood of the project.
» Data integrity is key.

(See Table 5.2.)

CARREFOUR

Carrefour have led the way in e-tailing with a system based on GNX: GlobalNetxchange. This is an electronic marketplace facilitating

Table 5.2 eHub Business Results (courtesy Sam Brown).

From	To
Fragmented processes	Single process
Disparate systems	One system – standards driven
Inconsistent application	Best practice driven
No visibility	Total end-to-end visibility across enterprises
Data quality – inaccuracy	Quality data – accurate and clean
High level of manual intervention	Predominantly automated processes
No real understanding of demand drivers	Understanding of all causal factors in demand management
No modeling/simulation capability	Full modeling "what if" and future planning capability
Multiple and inappropriate KPIs	Appropriate and fully trackable KPIs
Poor track record – inaccurate forecasting	Optimal accuracy and performance in forecasting and fulfillment

collaboration among retailers and suppliers globally. It is open to all retailers, wholesalers, and suppliers – neutrality is stressed, as is the need for confidentiality. Retailers and suppliers can become members of the exchange at "very minimal cost," so barriers to entry are low.

Carrefour have recognized that customer response is dependent on four major issues:

» communication;
» collaboration;
» connection; and
» synchronization.

It is the last, synchronization, that is the essential "value-add." Suppliers and retailers want improved efficiency and communication across the entire supply chain, together with visibility, lower costs, and lower inventory levels. They need access to new markets, and global as well as local sources. Whilst it is clear that EDI is still an extremely useful tool, small and medium enterprises (SMEs) in particular want reduced EDI and third party costs. And as all parts of the business are interconnected, enhanced business intelligence and management information should follow. It is possible that in this collaborative scenario, technology costs can be shared, and that new products can reach market more quickly.

For the consumers, the end result should be:

» better value;
» faster innovation;
» faster response (the product they want when they want it);
» global assortment;
» fresher products; and
» the ability to customize.

However, this will not happen unless all parties concerned take the matter of standards very seriously. Without standards, businesses cannot communicate. As there is more than one exchange and every seller is also a buyer, exchanges need to offer total interoperability. Unfortunately, there is not yet agreement, and there is no unified global organization to deliver relevant global standards. It is interesting to note that Cisco also emphasize this point, and have supported RosettaNet,[12] a self-funded, not-for-profit organization working to produce open e-business standards.

The other side of the coin is that building exchanges requires substantial re-engineering of internal systems and business approaches. It is most definitely a multistage process. E-enabling your business is a journey, not an event! It is best to start by getting connected! Then experiment with auctions, and gradually work towards a strategy of e-procurement. Think about your future EDI strategy, and explore the potential for collaboration with your best suppliers and customers. Set realistic targets, stay focused, and do not rush. You must focus on where you are going to get best value – where will you get most out of it. Members of exchanges have reported that there is a noticeable increase in learning and sharing, and a lot of communication between the visitors once they are set up.

Once again, this is a plea for "back to basics." It seems that all too often the fundamentals are not put into place in a systematic way.

E-BUSINESS WITHOUT TEARS

» Draw up and maintain an e-market strategy.
» Do not confuse business cases.
» Construct realistic business cases.
» Monitor and manage benefits.
» Take advantage of back-end integration.
» Keep your e-market options open.

NOTES

1 See, for example, www.globalisationguide.org.
2 Porter, M. (1998) "Clusters and the new economics of competition." *HBR*, November, pp. 77–90.
3 www.whatis.com.
4 Watkins, S. (2001) "E-commerce –The new agenda." *Logistics Solutions*, Issue 4, pp 29–32.
5 Magretta, J. (1998) "The power of virtual integration: An interview with Dell Computer's Michael Dell." *HBR*, March, pp. 73–84.
6 Barratt, M. (2001) "Mapping out the new world of e-business." E-logistics conference, Access International Conferences.
7 Many thanks to Sam Brown for permission to use material from one of his conference presentations: www.manugistics.com.
8 Evans, P. & Wurster, T. (1999) "Getting real about virtual commerce." *HBR*, November, pp. 85–94.
9 Bywater: www.bywater.co.uk.
10 http://www.covisint.com/.
11 Grosvenor, F. & Austin, T. (2001) "Cisco's eHub initiative." *Supply Chain Management Review*, July, pp. 28–35.
12 www.RosettaNet.org.

The State of the Art

The Internet has changed the way we do business, but other technologies are also involved. Here we look at a number of developments that will bring even greater changes:

- » software agents
- » virtual reality
- » simulation and business modeling
- » voice services
- » document management and workflow.

We have entered a new era. The Internet has changed the business paradigm and gives us new opportunities for working smarter. Wireless technologies are opening up new channels for business services. The Internet and information technologies are drivers for:

» disintermediation – closer customer contact;
» immediacy – real-time commerce and cycle-time compression;
» workgroups – data-sharing and communication;
» digitization – fluidity of data and innovation;
» globalization – universal passport to information; and
» mobility – any information, anywhere.

From large computer systems with complex software in the 1970s, we have moved to ubiquitous, networked computer systems with many tools and applications to make them easier to use. It is not just a new way of working – it is a new way of doing business. Just as managers think they understand the impact of new technologies, new developments overtake them. The acceleration effect – the ever-increasing speed of change – is overwhelming. Everyone is now online. Everyone shares information. Business intelligence gathering is critical, but everyone is becoming more efficient. You have to find more creative ways to use your technology to stay ahead of your competitors. Research into integration and voice services is now a priority to allow workers to be truly "location independent." New channels are expected to emerge and customers in the networked society have greater expectations and increased demand for services that are:

» fun;
» add value and enhance work;
» easy to access and use;
» personalized;
» relevant; and
» time critical.

The technological requirements for each type of worker vary, but include e-mail and voice mail; document management and workflow systems; work scheduling systems; route planning and database access. Details can be found on many Websites.[1]

For business success, technology has to be turned into business solutions. It is appropriate in this chapter to include some technical applications that continue to impact the way we work and design organizations: software agents, virtual reality, simulation, process modeling, security, developments in voice recognition and natural language, and workflow and groupware solutions.

VIRTUAL ASSISTANTS

A fascinating new technology is the development of intelligent software agents. You can think of them as "electronic butlers." Some applications have been developed as Personal Digital Assistants (PDAs) – software programs coded to do things for you. Imagine the enormous amounts of time that could be saved: access to a PDA to help you in your business research means that an agent would search the Web and report back with the references whilst you were getting on with something else.

One manager interviewed thought that intelligent agents referred to his call center staff! There is a lot to learn about this technology. It has been around for a long time, evolving out of the early artificial intelligence (AI) research. The lack of a single definition, and the jargon and acronyms that abound in this subject, make it a specialist study. Yet we are already very dependent on such agents. Here are two definitions found on the Internet:

> "An agent is a software thing that knows how to do things that you could probably do yourself if you had the time."
> *Ted Selker, IBM Almaden Research Center*

> "A piece of software which performs a given task using information gleaned from its environment to act in a suitable manner so as to complete the task successfully. The software should be able to adapt itself based on changes occurring in its environment, so that a change in circumstances will still yield the intended result."[2]

Another name for agents is software robots (bots for short).[3] They are increasingly important when we use the Internet and are already employed in processes as diverse as air traffic control, information retrieval, scheduling, diary management, and workflow. A mail bot filters junk mail from e-mail. A "spider" is a mobile Web agent that roams networks to retrieve documents and index information. There is a lot of work on the use of agents for e-commerce:

» home shopping with filtering and recommendation capabilities; and
» targeted and intelligent promotion techniques based on consumer preferences.[4]

One reason for the growth in interest in agent-based computing in business is the development of a new generation of "collaborative" agents. Intelligent enough to act autonomously, they are able to plan and negotiate with other agents to achieve shared objectives. The author has been investigating the potential for these agents to aid the development of self-managed teams: they would provide an excellent communication channel, but would be a means of reassuring senior management that the teams were not "doing their own thing." A lot more work is needed before we can go that far, but already trials are being carried out to use such agents to broker services between people. Broker agents might contain details of specific skills or competency requirements, then track down and negotiate with agents carrying resource information to plan the most effective staffing or scheduling of a project.

Agent technology could play an important role in supporting both lone workers and virtual organizations. This cannot happen without compatible computing and mobile devices, and internationally agreed software standards and protocols.[5]

Can you imagine delegating work to a computer and trusting it to make choices for you? At work we have to trust our colleagues to act on our behalf. Now we will have to learn to manage and trust our agents. For many people, that will mean increasing their level of computer literacy. Yet, in the long term, agent technology has the potential to create a step change in the way we work and manage. (See Fig. 6.1.)

VIRTUAL REALITY

Many people associate virtual organization with virtual reality. The technologies can be used as enablers for business but are not generally

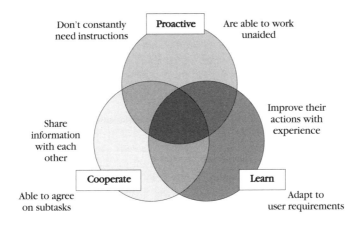

Fig. 6.1 Software agents: key attributes. (Courtesy of John Shepherdson.)

about "organization." In a world of accelerating business change, we need all the help we can get!

It is claimed that Jaron Lanier coined the term "virtual reality" in 1986, but interpretations vary. It is now more common (and useful) to discuss "virtual environments." Military personnel might use the term "synthetic environment." The Virtual Reality Society[6] is dedicated to the advancement of this discipline and related technologies.

Virtual reality is about immersion, interactivity, and information intensity. Boot et al.[7] wrote that:

> "A final product of information technology at present appears bizarre ... this is virtual reality ... The clearest impact of virtual reality will be in business."

They also wrote that perhaps we lack the imagination to recognize "new forms of living and working together" and it seems as if we are stuck in the existing template for the concept "organization."

Although it is still regarded as bizarre by many people, virtual reality has already become a part of our life just as many other technologies have quickly become commonplace. Peter Cochrane,[8] formerly Head of Research at BT's Martlesham Laboratories, is fascinated by the power of technology. He believes that virtual reality has an important part to play in business, as "it is ideally suited to the representation of highly complex and data-rich situations. Visualizing the operational information of a company is far more edifying than a spreadsheet." If you could use virtual reality tools to aid decision-making, think of the cost savings for managers at all levels.

Every company wants to achieve "right first time, every time." But traditionally, that meant experimentation, prototyping, and reiteration until we got it right. Now we can use "virtuality" to help us to reduce those iterations. Cochrane sees virtual reality as an aid to just-in-time: it can reduce time to market and help to get products right first time. He suggests that "visualizing the final design in virtual operation is vital in getting it right, but without the expense of an actual build." In his remarkable book *108 Tips for Time Travellers*, Cochrane lists medical and surgical applications, repairs of oil refineries, and teaching science, all within the remit of virtual reality. Mathematical functions "no longer have to be artificially frozen in time and space by the limitation of paper, but can be alive with n-dimensional interactivity."

Most of us cannot yet access the virtual reality experience as we do not have the computer power to do so, but business organizations are certainly aware of the potential of these technologies.

SIMULATION AND BUSINESS PROCESS MODELING

Simulation is a particular type of modeling. Gilbert and Troitzsch[9] give a useful explanation of the difference between statistical and simulation models.

If an initial design is flawed, be it for a product or a service, there will be problems during manufacture, production, and delivery. Costs will rise due to events such as corrective action, arguments between staff, the need to deal with customer complaints, and repair and/or replacement activities. If we can simulate the processes before we move to production, many of the problems can be avoided. By using such modeling techniques, we can try to build in risk prevention and defect elimination.

Using simulation for process improvement has a long history. Many people associate simulation with the training of pilots and flight simulators. In business it was initially confined to manufacturing and research and development functions. From the early 1990s it became more widespread as business process re-engineering (BPR) became popular. Managers realized that processes must be simplified before new automated systems were installed.

The potential to study the interaction of many variables and to carry out "what if" scenarios led to insights into problems that could not be solved through more conventional methods. Proctor[10] discusses the application of simulation to problems of queuing and bottlenecks; Richardson[11] linked simulation and systems thinking. He suggested that the goal of modeling work is to support planning, policy analysis, and strategic decision-making. The usefulness of formal models is to provide quantitative tools to "reduce uncertainty, disagreement and complexity."

In contrast, Ould[12] and his colleagues have designed a method primarily for qualitative analysis. They do not believe that every situation requires a radical business change. Their method involves roles, activities which produce and operate on entities, and which communicate, coordinate, and collaborate through interactions.

The development of sophisticated software applications speeds up the process and makes it more manageable. The danger in all simulations is that IT specialists or managers carry out the work without the input of the people who actually do the work. Wildberger[13] presents a succinct overview of the development of simulation, in which he draws attention to the fact that:

> "Basing management decisions on a simulation's output makes sense only if the simulation model includes all the factors and activities that affect the goals of those decisions. Today's modelling tools ignore many of these factors and activities, especially those with significant behavioural and cognitive content."

According to his work, issues that are rarely addressed include:

» sharing supply and demand information at the appropriate level;
» deciding how to share a scarce resource;

» using negotiation and compromise mechanisms to synchronize suppliers and/or distributors;
» avoiding "arms races" – price wars, feature inflation, attempts at market control;
» determining a fair way to share risk;
» making goals explicit for all levels of responsibility.

To avoid the mechanistic models, Wildberger suggests a bottom-up modeling approach, including the use of multiple adaptive agents. These simulations can then be used as "flight trainers" for managers.

SECURITY

Security issues are becoming increasingly important as more traffic is moved onto the Internet. Prevention of unauthorized access has led to a proliferation of security methods. This is a brief overview, included for completeness. It is an area where state-of-the-art technologies are leading to some extraordinary developments.[14]

Peter Cochrane[15] writes that "ultimately the weak link is the people involved, and it may be some time before machines can outsmart us." He draws attention to the cost of sophisticated methods, but if you use a series of techniques in succession he suggests that "super-security can be both low cost and convenient."

Firewalls, passwords, and smart cards are commonly used for security, but are not considered sufficiently secure for financial transactions or for verifying the identity of parties wishing to access confidential information. Encryption – the scrambling of the message – is often used, but biotechnology is being developed to find a unique identifier for each user.

BioPassword[16] allows access after two factors have been authenticated. The user must know the correct user name and password, but the typing rhythm must match a template that has been stored in the system. Sophisticated methods include face, voice, hand, and fingerprint recognition, and other biometrics are under development. Speaker verification is a strong biometric that has been tested with professional imitators. These systems work in most cases, but not with twins or close siblings. For those groups, retina scanning is a possibility, but invasive techniques are not popular.

Disparate Internet initiatives must be aligned to avoid commercial chaos. Acceptance of electronic signatures is an important example of this. The UK is one of the first countries in the world to pass legislation in this area, and the Electronic Signatures Directive became law in July 2001. This is significant, as the traditional means of authenticating contracts – signatures on forms – is a major obstacle to electronic commerce.

VOICE SERVICES

Some of the most irritating interfaces for customers are the interactive voice response (IVR) systems, first developed in the 1980s, and now common in call centers. Waiting for a disembodied voice to deliver a message can be a waste of time as well as frustrating. Phoneme-based speech recognition systems were piloted in the late 1990s. Phonemes are the audible syllables of the ee/aa/uu sounds. In the USA there are nine different phoneme sets (dialects). In the UK there are 19 sets, not including Irish or Northern Irish sets.

This work led to more advanced systems of natural language understanding (NLU). These systems allow you to give a long string of instructions, and include a "barge-in" facility. This means that when a person speaks over the automated prompts, the system can cope and not crash. Text-to-speech is already used to read back e-mail messages for instance. This is an obvious advantage for a mobile worker who does not wish to go back to the office to collect messages.

Another development is the ability to talk to your computer. Voice recognition software is sufficiently advanced to allow you to:

"dictate entire paragraphs at a time. Compose e-mail messages, create reports, draft letters, and edit proposals just by speaking."

It is claimed that you can also edit and format a document by voice commands.

The aim of several research groups is to develop more natural conversational applications, including convergence with Web technologies. Nuance and Mitel are two companies involved in this work. You might find that when you log on to a site, you see a "persona" who talks to you as if you are speaking to a real person. At present the demonstrations of such applications suffer from the jerkiness of the voices and stilted animations of the figures – rather like the video links from remote locations you see on TV news programs.

The Internet was not designed for voice and video. Gateways have to be designed to link PCs, telephones, and fax machines with the Internet. Voice over IP[17] (voice delivered over the Internet) is bringing down the costs of multimedia transfer so that there is a deluge of new products and services. Unified messaging is bringing the convergence of all communications systems – e-mail, voicemail, and fax – into a common inbox that can be accessed anywhere, from whichever channel you wish to use.[18]

DOCUMENT MANAGEMENT AND WORKFLOW SYSTEMS

One of the most important facets of virtual organization is the movement of data and control of documents. We used to associate document management with libraries. Now we talk of databases, data mining, and warehousing. Anyone working virtually must have access to relevant information when required and in the appropriate format. This applies whether employees are co-located in different sections within one building or comprise a distributed workforce working in the same country or in distant parts of the world.

An obvious example of this is the use of call centers for "front-office" operations. The customer service advisors (or agents as they are sometimes called) require many different kinds of information when a customer telephones. The customer wants a "one-stop" shop, expecting the person who answers his or her query to know the case history, financial details, and so on. It is very frustrating if you have to repeat details every time you contact a company or if they pass you on to a different department. In practice, the internal software systems of most companies are not integrated. The information might be held on legacy systems; filed in a traditional filing cabinet; held on a computer system in a different department; kept in an e-mail file; on the system but not up-to-date. The variations are many and diverse.

To overcome this kind of problem, document management systems, scanning devices, and workflow solutions have been under development for many years. The potential of integrated workflow and information management is still not achieved, as suppliers are still arguing over standards that will promote interoperability. Despite the demands of customers, some suppliers are still protecting their proprietary systems, rather than pooling "intellectual property." The Workflow Management Coalition[19] is a key player in these developments.

GROUPWARE

Closely linked to workflow are the concepts of groupware and other applications developed for cooperative work. The term "groupware" covers a number of software applications that aid teamwork. Such applications are designed to facilitate work amongst people who are not co-located, and as such are an important element in the development of virtual organizations. Computer-supported cooperative work (CSCW) is the name given to the study of computer systems supporting teamwork. Terms associated with these studies include Workgroup Computing and Technological Support for Work Group Collaboration.

Groupware technologies are typically categorized[20] as co-located/different place and synchronous/asynchronous. (See Table 6.1.)

Table 6.1

	Same time Synchronous	**Different time** Asynchronous
Same place Co-located	Voting Presentation Support	Shared computers
Different place Distance	Videophones Chat lines	E-mail Workflow

HEALTH WARNING!

» IT can provide information overload. This then leads to over-analysis and overmeasurement to the extent that managers can become distracted by data so much that they forget the people.

» Electronic communication is so immediate that it can drive managers to constantly change arrangements – leading to more stress, more change, less in-depth knowledge, understanding and project completion.

» IT can make supplier–customer relationships "antiseptic." We have to counter "lack of love" feeling by putting people back on a face-to-face basis (rather than interface).

» Many employees (especially managers) are under pressure to be IT compatible/dependent so as to "prove" their efficiency and modern progressive outlook or culture.

NOTES

1 See, for example, dialspace.dial.pipex.com/mda www.sectec. co.uk/wired/bp6.htm and www.the-rfg.com/telecom/reprints/ starvox/1026tn.html.

2 www.hermans.org/agents/h22.htm.

3 http://seminars.internet.com/bot/sf01/agenda.html.

4 Tepsidis, I. *et al*. (1997) *The Potential of Electronic Commerce*: http://agents.www.media.mit.edu/people/moux/papers/emm-sec97.pdf.

5 For further discussion see articles found at http://leap.crm-paris. com/.

6 www.vrs.org.uk.

7 Boot, R. *et al*. (1994) *Managing the Unknown by Creating New Futures*. McGraw-Hill, London.

8 Cochrane, P. (1997) *108 Tips for Time Travellers*. Orion, London.

9 Gilberg, N. & Troitzsch, K. (1999) *Simulation for the Social Scientist*. Open University Press, Buckingham.

10 Proctor, R. (1994) "Simulation in management services." *Management Services*, January, pp. 18–21.

11 Richardson, G. (1996) *Modelling for Management* (Vols I & II). Dartmouth Publishing, Aldershot.

12 Ould, M. (1995) *Business Processes – Modelling and Analysis for Re-engineering and Improvement*. Wiley.

13 Wildberger, A.M. (2000) "AI and simulation." *Simulation*, September, pp. 171–72.

14 A lot of information is available on the Internet. See also textbooks such as Columbus, L. (1999) *Administrator's Guide to E-commerce*. Prompt, Indianapolis.

15 Cochrane, P. (1997) *108 Tips for Time Travellers*. Orion, London.

16 www.biopassword.com.

17 A comprehensive overview can be found at www.cis.ohio-state.edu. See also Tyler, G. (2001). "Voice and IP finally getting together?" *Management Services*, February, pp 18–23.

18 See, for example, www.mitel.com.

19 www.aiim.org/wfmc/mainframe.ftm.

20 Taken from www.usabilityfirst.com/groupware/intro.txl.

Success Stories

Practical examples are plentiful; typical cases are not. Here we examine four examples of good practice:

- » Pentacle The Virtual Business School
- » Lands' End
- » HSBC
- » BT.

The good news is that there are many companies that have successfully experimented with virtual organization. Trying to choose "typical" cases is impossible. Here are four totally diverse case studies, each of which demonstrates the innovative use of technology to reinvent their businesses.

The first case is about Pentacle The Virtual Business School,[1] illustrating the revolution in the way in which companies are handling their training needs. It is based on an interview with Eddie Obeng, well known throughout the world for his "New World" thinking. This complements the discussion in Chapter 4 on virtual universities.

E-business (Chapter 5) is the subject of the next two cases. Lands' End[2] demonstrates the potential of virtual shopping. The ways in which the Web can be used to add customer value, making it a fun way to shop rather than just an online catalogue, are well illustrated.

Online banking has been chosen to illustrate the changes in the financial sector. HSBC[3] were the first to set up a telephone banking system, and are now expanding their Web-based operations.

Virtual teams (discussed in Chapter 8) are most commonly associated with virtual organization, and the case from BT[4] shows how a high-tech solution can provide new levels of customer service.

Especial thanks to Eddie Obeng (Pentacle The Virtual Business School), Bert Kolz (Lands' End), Matthew Higgins (HSBC), and John Shepherdson (BT).

PENTACLE THE VIRTUAL BUSINESS SCHOOL

If you examine the way educational institutions are run, you discover that few processes in those organizations are actually to do with learning. Many processes are about administration and nonteaching activities. Why, then, do you need large business schools?

At business schools, lecturers traditionally teach a number of faculty-based subjects, but such a structure does not suit changing client demands. How can you break down that framework? A very well run hierarchy cannot be easily changed from within, as the whole point of the hierarchy is to maintain the status quo. Most organizations are designed so that learning is actually very effective. People learn a few things very effectively, then repeat them. The learning spreads out through the organization, but if you want to change it, you have to help them to unlearn. One way to make progress is to build a new organization and a new way of working, and grow that.

Eddie Obeng realized that people wanted to learn continuously, rather than on a "one-off" basis. Why send people away to college for four weeks? Can you make courses shorter? Can you make them modular? Ideally, you want people to learn continuously and to apply their new learning as they go along.

Eddie Obeng therefore decided to try out a new model. He set out to provide new learning in a new way. He reasoned that in the "New World," much of the content that people are learning is obsolete. Traditional ways of teaching strategy are also often irrelevant. You have to look at two key elements:

» the actual learning of an individual; and
» how to organize internally to deliver it.

If you want to encourage continuous learning, you need to use technology. You can use the classroom model, but when people go back to work, they want to keep talking to you. Groupware solutions provide support, but you need a mixture of technologies, and have to learn which is most appropriate at each interaction. It will depend on what you are trying to communicate. Why not put boring tutors online as they are only dealing with content, and have classroom learning for giving support and motivation and stimulation?

If there is a high emotional content, or if it is complex, or if interaction is essential before people understand, you need a 1:1 situation. Technology should not be used for such situations. E-mails have a low emotional content and usually the messages are simple. The telephone is a technology for relatively high emotion/relatively complex messages. Audio-conferencing is only useful for less complex issues, as so many people are involved. At Pentacle they rarely use video-conferencing, as people cannot receive it at their desks. People want to learn *locally*. In a global organization the time zone difference can also be a problem.

This raises an interesting point about *distance learning*. That is part of the old mindset, because the learning is seen as distant from the *provider*. Classroom learning is local learning from the learners' point of view. Now you have to think about where they want to learn;

what support they want at work; whether or not they are online; and whether they can cope with multimedia offerings. You need to design learning from the student's point of view.

At Pentacle there is just 2,800 sq. ft. of space and five core staff. Everything that can be is outsourced. One company meets clients at the airport; another delivers computers when they are needed; one does the photocopying; another takes phone messages. As an organization, this has the impact of a large company, but it is virtual.

The internal framework allows flexibility. There is a "virtual faculty" which allows the School to focus on the needs of the clients. Staff change according to the courses being provided. According to Eddie Obeng, past clients make good tutors, as they understand the New World from a practical point of view!

It is not just a matter of "empowering" people to work differently. Good practice changes, and if you empower people to use their good ideas, there is a fair chance that those ideas could be bad business. It is not enough to empower people. You must also give them the capability to understand how business survives and thrives in this New World. That part of the training is too often ignored. There may be lip service, but it is not done thoroughly.

Eddie Obeng has an interesting perspective on cultural issues in a virtual world. He sums it up as "fair = different." (This is fully explained in his book *New Rules for the New World*). You need to find a way into the hearts and minds of your people. If you are a team leader in a virtual team, you need ways of engaging people. There must be two-way "conversations," and there must be some output. You cannot have just one style, because you have a moving team, with different personalities at different times, and you need to do different things for them. (This kind of thinking would make you a more effective leader in both a virtual and a "normal" team.)

In Pentacle's Business Faculty, every project has a different team. There have to be certain ground rules, including the technology being used. People are brought in on a need basis, as projects grow. Traditional teams suffer many interruptions and problems. You need to apply the same disciplines, but as virtual teams are more complex, you have to be clear on the concept of stakeholders. This is key. Who is going to be affected by what you are doing? If you are the team leader, you need to be able to map out the involvement of each stakeholder. Which members comprise the core team? Facing that problem helps you to work out who should be in that core team.

It does not matter what you call them – you may use the phrase virtual team, but many people think that if you use that phrase it is not a "real" team. It is certainly distributed, but by that do you mean through time, or geographically, or both? When you think about it, traditional teams were never of one type. Many people use sporting teams as an analogy, but just think about the differences between a cricket team, rugby team, football team and so on. The role of the captain, the roles of the team members, all contribute in different ways in different types of team.

Eddie Obeng clarifies this by defining a team as a group of people who have three things:

1 a common goal – we all understand what we are trying to achieve;
2 some level of interdependence, and belief that we cannot win unless the others do; and
3 a feeling that if we make a mistake, other people will notice.

If those three elements are in place, you have a team. Senior managers will often quote members of the organization who they think are in their team, but if these three elements are missing, it is just not true, with or without the use of technology. The technology means that you have to be cleverer about how you do it. You have to take more care about defining the stakeholders and how you set the ground rules.

Eddie Obeng discovered that the economics of working as a virtual business school are very different. Traditional schools depend on long programs for cash flow and have many overheads. The virtual school has low fixed costs and high variable costs due to many short programs, many of them online. It is a very different model, but is working well. Most of the clients are large and successful companies. They come to Pentacle because they are looking for something different, and are often from the more innovative parts of these companies (i.e. not the mainstream business). They come to learn what things they have to change. One of the most important things they learn is that in the New World, the moneymaking process is more important than the control processes that dominated the Old World. Eddie Obeng acknowledges that teaching people about the New World, virtual or not, is a journey to a new way of thinking.

LEARNING POINTS FOR VIRTUAL LEARNING

» 90% of what people know is probably obsolete.

» Be patient. People do not buy into everything all at once. They many go away and not return for two or three years. They come back when they begin to recognize the power of the new thinking.

» Use a Socratic approach to learning. Help people to realize things for themselves. Many of the people you teach are smarter than you are. Turn the learning process on its head. Build consensus and discuss alternatives, rather than stand up and deliver "answers."

» Be aware of people's fear and build relationships with people. Too many people still use the old ways of teaching – "Let me tell you what I know" – which then has no impact.

» Start with small teams, developing new ones when you need more people. Take care to find out who are the stakeholders.

» Trust becomes a very important issue.

» The process used must be appropriate. If you have not taught people how to change, you will increase resistance to change instead of helping them to move on.

» Break the force of tradition. People brought up in the Old World do not respect their own learning. They reason: I thought of that, so the idea cannot be any good. That is another cycle that has to be broken.

» Classroom learning has an important part to play to reinforce learning.

LANDS' END: VIRTUAL SHOPPING

To stay competitive, it is not sufficient to put a catalog online. Successful use of the Internet means finding innovative ways of doing business that add value for the customer. In the light of the dotcom crashes in

2000–2001, it is particularly interesting to follow the success of Lands' End.

Bert Kolz, manager, international e-commerce, believes that the company's success stems from its ability to overcome the challenges of fulfillment. It sees the key success factors as:

» excellent Website navigation and use;
» interactive shopping aids;
» telephone center integration;
» reliable order processing; and
» state of the art warehousing.

Lands' End is an international direct merchant of classic clothing for men, women, and children. With headquarters in Dodgeville, WI, there are subsidiaries in the UK, Germany, and Japan. 14% of sales come from outside the USA.

There are no brick and mortar operations in Ireland, France, or Italy – those countries are supplied from offices in the UK or Germany. The UK warehouse services the whole of Europe.

TIMELINE
» **1995**: US site launched.
» **1998** (fiscal year): US sales reach $18mn.
» **1999**: UK, Germany, and Japan sites launched.
» **2001**: UK and Germany have virtual model.
» **2001**: ''Lands' End Custom.''
» **2001** (fiscal year): US sales reach $218mn.

The accolades won by the Lands' End operations bear tribute to their success. They are particularly proud of winning the European Web-enabled Call Center of the Year award, a testimony to their use of new technologies combined with a dedication to customer service excellence. Patricia Seybold also rated them a #1 e-commerce site; and in 2000 they were inducted into the Smithsonian Institute and were awarded a Revolution Pioneer Award.

Everything they do online they plan in terms of site navigation. All through the Website, alternative products are shown. This is one way to develop user-friendly offerings. They offer a complete set of complementary merchandise, which also reduces inconvenience for their customers. Each home page is tailored to the country for which it is intended. The welcome page must catch the attention of the customer, present an opportunity to sell thousands of items, yet must not look cluttered. Separating items into categories such as men's, ladies', and children's wear is one simple way to help customers.

Once an item is selected, accessories that go with that item are illustrated. Illustrations of similar items are also automatically shown, saving yet more time searching for alternatives. On one side of the page will be a list of headings, to make navigation to other items easy. Different colors, sizes, textures, and other options are shown, and a series of buttons make ordering easy. There is an online messaging system that indicates if there is a delivery delay or if the item is out of stock, so that customers do not waste time putting the item into the shopping trolley.

A winning formula for this site is the addition of interactive shopping aids:

» body scanning;
» virtual model;
» Lands' End Custom; and
» shop with a friend.

An interesting experiment for Lands' End is the *body scan*. Booths are set up in all the major cities in the USA. You go into a cubicle, change into a two-piece outfit supplied by the company, then walk into the bio-scanning booth. A safe light scans the body in 12 seconds. The data from this scan produces a virtual model, which customers can see online by entering their password.

Once the virtual model is available, style advice can be offered. When you choose a sweater, for example, it is shown on your own body model. When you see the sweater, the software adds pants and other items. Whole outfits can be illustrated. If you want a color or texture check, the company will send a free swatch. It even offers a monogramming and hemming service.

After the pilot, the company discovered that it could be inconvenient for the customer to travel to the booth to get the scan, so to improve the service it has introduced a new experiment in the USA – *Lands' End Custom*. This will not provide the perfect fit, but the fit will be better than buying clothes off the rack. Ease of use for the customer is a critical success factor for Lands' End, and this trial run is yet another example of trying to provide what the customer wants.

Shop with a friend means that people in any part of the world can connect online and shop together. One of the pleasures of shopping is the social experience – so Lands' End tries to imitate that by using technology to bring people together to shop virtually. Offering an online option is a natural extension of the catalog business, and many men in particular who do not like shopping find this a quick and easy way to purchase goods.

Call centers are a key element in this service. The company has to evaluate how to integrate its complete service offering. Customers might contact it through telephone, fax, e-mail or the Websites. When a customer calls in, they expect the company's advisors to know their case history and to give a personal service. All the call center staff have been trained to support the Websites as well as dealing with telephone inquiries. They might get thousands of e-mails a day, and the standard response time is to answer within three hours.

A new development is real-time text chat (*Lands' End Live*), which is very popular. All these contact points are clearly stated on the Website, offering a customer full choice. No special software or downloads are needed, and the customer can be guided through the site – the advisor and customer can surf the site together. The advisor can even split the screen and illustrate other items – an opportunity to cross-sell. If the customer has a second telephone line, they can talk during this surfing. If there is none, you can text chat, which is particularly popular in the USA.

To further reassure customers, there is e-mail confirmation of order and shipment, with two-day standard delivery. Customers can track orders online, and there is an unconditional guarantee. If you buy anything from Lands' End, and want to return it, there is no time limit and no conditions attached.

Reliable shipping depends on good relationships with the carriers. The core competence of Lands' End is the business of selling product to consumers, not distribution. The company develops close partnerships with the carriers so that they can work out their strategies together, including a strategy for returned goods – a key feature of the online shopping scene.

Last but not least, Lands' End looks after the needs of its employees, who are seen as the backbone of the company. The many long-term service records in the company are a testimony to its success.

KEY POINTS

» Personal service.
» 100% customer focus.
» Strategies are driven by customer demand.
» Strategies must reflect the local market.
» Presentation is only a small fraction of the game.
» Make it easy for customers to contact the company.
» Constantly look for ways to cater for customer demand and expectations.

HSBC: THE UNBANK-LIKE BANK

The strategy of HSBC was to set up First Direct as a virtual bank from the outset. Whilst First Direct remains a UK-based operation, it is ideally suited as a case study. HSBC is one of the largest banks in the world, and is ready to expand globally: it is well placed for expansion into both the USA and Europe.

TIMELINE

» **1988**: Project "Raincloud" was launched by Midland Bank (as it was until taken over by HSBC) and within a year became "First Direct."
» **1989**: Officially launched at midnight, Sunday, October 1. This was deliberate, to emphasize the new service proposition: 24 hour banking, 7 days a week.
» **1997**: Nearly 800,000 customers had signed up.
» **1998**: PC banking introduced.

> » **January 2001**: Independent financial service launched.
> » **June 2001**: Smart-mortgage account launched.
> » **2001–2003**: WAP technologies likely to be superseded by 3G.

In the late 1980s UK clearing banks had a very poor reputation for customer service. The traditional relationship between bank and customer was that of parent/child, with banks acting as old-fashioned patrons, or rather like a Victorian patriarch. Customers were regarded as a necessary evil, and were generally treated as a nuisance. First Direct sought to turn this situation on its head, treating customers as like-minded equals, seeking their input into the way the bank was run and generally behaving in a completely "unbank-like" manner.

To achieve the new goals, there was a need to get rid of some of the traditional obstacles to customer service: queues, limited opening hours or finding a place to park, for instance. The solution was to use more convenient, portable, and ever-accessible means of communication, while maintaining person-to-person contact. This led inevitably to telephone banking: nearly everybody has a phone, and everybody is used to using it as an effective communication tool.

Crucially, the idea of creating this new "unbank-like" bank – the idea of an iconoclastic brand, of being nonconformist – came first. The telephone was simply the tool, but it worked, and it worked extremely well. Many "early adopters" were busy professionals, already heavy users of electronic services such as the Internet, and willing to embrace labor and time-saving devices and methods.

When First Direct went on to introduce PC banking, the key challenge to overcome was to make sure that the systems "talked" to each other. Another was to ensure that banking representatives could follow each customer's interactions with the bank, whatever the medium. If a customer has banked on the telephone, the Internet banking system must recognize this, and vice versa.

The bank worked closely with a panel of customers to develop the PC banking service, working with them almost as consultants, making sure that the customer view was fully represented. The system had to be reliable, functional, and have good design and content. A phased roll-out was chosen so that customers could be gradually introduced to an efficient and aesthetically pleasing Website, and a PC banking service that fulfilled expectations. At the time of writing, 400,000 customers (out of a base of one million) have taken up the service. They utilize Internet banking, but as a complement to the telephone service, rather than as an alternative. Customers have the opportunity to use a multichannel banking service, which now includes telephone, Internet, and mobile phone text messaging services.

KEY LEARNING POINTS

» Staff attitudes are crucial. On the telephone, they behave as like-minded people with customers, rather than as bankers talking at customers. This enables them to build up a rapport with customers from an early stage, to the extent that surveys show that the service they receive over the phone was much better and more personal than that which they had previously received over the counter at a bank branch.

» Personal service is not conditional on face-to-face contact. First Direct has helped to make telephone contact the "new face-to-face service" in financial services, making the quality of the conversation of utmost importance.

» Financial products are much the same from any provider, but the way in which they are offered and serviced varies enormously. First Direct has had the most satisfied customers in the UK for over a decade now, and has also been the UK's most recommended bank for the same period of time.

» Telephone and Web are complementary channels. The Web is expanding enormously for day-to-day banking, with balances, money movements, and bill payments fast becoming the norm for younger, more upmarket and financially astute people. It is likely to be some time before people buy more complex products over the Web, such as mortgages, pensions, and investments, although the innovators and early adopters are already beginning to show some interest in doing this.

» The telephone is becoming the new "face-to-face." HSBC prides itself on its one-to-one personal banking service. Since the launch nearly 12 years ago, customers have always spoken to a person, and in spite of new technologies, HSBC says that it intends to keep it this way. Many customers find the service more personal than that they used to receive from their local branch, but this is probably more to do with the nature of the conversation. There is a much more friendly and informal relationship between bank and customer. The bank realized early on that the interactive voice response (IVR) systems are unpopular, and customers are greeted at once by a person, who then if necessary reroutes the call after finding out the requirements. Fully automated systems are perceived as being designed solely for business benefits, rather than for the customers.

» It is becoming an alternative to branch banking, and many find it quicker, more convenient, and a better use of their time. For the majority of customers, the need for face-to-face contact is minimal.

BT UK

Following privatization in 1984, BT had to adapt quickly to the new environment: demands of shareholders; regulation by Oftel; market forces including globalization; and increased customer expectations. At the same time, technology was increasing the *rate* of change. BT had to develop a new way of working to meet these new demands. The problem was to provide better levels of customer service, whilst developing a lean administration. Efficient management of the engineering workforce became a critical success factor. It seemed unlikely that reliance on the old manual systems would allow new business targets to be met: manual controls could not cope with the new complexities. New business targets included the following.

» Business repair jobs must be cleared the same day if reported before 4 p.m.
» Residential repair jobs must be cleared the same day if reported before 1 p.m.
» Business repair work clearance within five hours of reporting.

» Residential repair work clearance within nine hours of reporting.
» Provision (of new equipment) on demand – two-hour appointment slots are offered.

BT developed virtual teams as a means to improve customer service and relationships, especially for the provision and repair operations in telecommunications. Their virtual team comprises:

» the account/sales team;
» the service team;
» the engineering/field team; and
» the marketing team.

(See Fig. 7.1.)

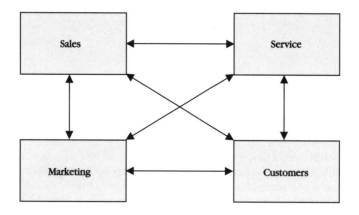

Fig. 7.1

These teams are geographically distributed and communicate via telephone, e-mail, internal customer service systems, and Internet-based systems via laptops. The service teams are mainly based in call centers, and need integrated systems so that information is quickly passed on to the appropriate member of staff.

Customers require a seamless operation – whoever they contact, they expect their personal details and case history to be on hand. Too often there are multiple contact points and even the team members can be confused about the correct procedures and responsibilities. To overcome this, a merger of cultures has been a critical success factor. Engineers and sales personnel have totally different perspectives on the problems. The company decided that the engineers, who have most frequent contact with customers, were to become the "face of the company." This need to enhance customer service in the light of increasing competition was the driver behind the technological solutions developed by BT. Key points they had to address included the following.

» Get the right person with the right skills to the right place at the right time.
» The concept of a work allocation system for a distributed (virtual) engineering team (BT has about 20,000 mobile employees who receive work in this way).
» Business and cultural factors influencing the design of the system.
» Reactions from the workforce to the new way of working.

Operational design in this case involved the specification and delivery of a computing function which fully automates the flow of work: from a customer request, to receipt by a field engineer and the automation of the closure flow, back to originating host systems including time recording and pay systems. Design and build work began in 1989 with the system starting operational trials in December 1991. The system has continued to evolve with the more recent development of dynamic scheduling and data visualization systems which have replaced the real time algorithm, automation of many supporting processes and a completely re-engineered laptop PC field system exploiting the latest Internet and wireless communications technologies (implemented in 2000–2001). The system not only achieved its original objectives – by 1999 it was delivering an annual operating cost reduction of £100mn together with improved customer service. The name given to this system is "Work Manager."

(See Fig. 7.2.)

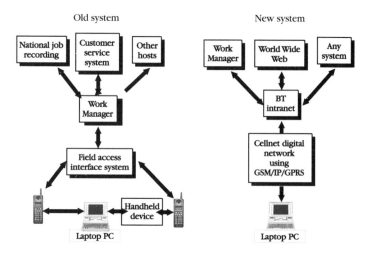

Fig. 7.2

Work Manager (WM) is an integrated allocation and field dispatch software system developed by BT to address their operational problems with improved field and control efficiency, reduced operating costs, improved customer service, and reliable management information. Using this system, work is generated and automatically allocated to a field engineer whose skills match the job to be done. The engineer used to receive the information via a rugged hand-held computer terminal, but now all engineers have laptop computers. An enhanced allocation system, dynamic scheduling, has dramatically improved the quality of service through greater optimization and visibility of the allocation process.

It is important to allow sufficient time for different types of job. Every type of work that goes through the system has a time allocated for that type of job. If the job requires knowledge of a new technology, a realistic provision time might be three to four hours. The latest software builds a schedule of work for each engineer, up until the day of the job and for the next seven days. Quite a lot of work will come in advance, so a future schedule can be built for each engineer. Gaps will probably be left for last-minute work. That is a static schedule. On the day the work is to be done, it turns into a dynamic schedule: most of the repair work is dealt with on the day it is reported, and is fitted into the static schedule virtually in real time.

The system works on the assumption that engineers will complete their work in the allotted time. If a job takes longer, the schedule must be recalculated. For that reason, the schedules are rerun every 15 minutes, to take account of the changing circumstances: a customer is out; the job is more complex than reported; stores have to be ordered. To achieve optimum scheduling, the algorithms are extremely complex.

For a company such as BT to provide the speedy service expected by customers, they have to adopt an entrepreneurial culture. In the short term, that will be exceedingly difficult, as current operations are controlled by an automated, sophisticated management system. Without Work Manager, the volumes of work and the service targets (required by the regulator Oftel as well as driven by competition) could not be achieved. However, as management policies evolve, the focus will be on more customer "self-service" through the Internet and other technologies, leading to yet more emphasis on the mobile field work-force as the "face" of BT. The need is to provide more flexible tools for those engineers, and to devise an appropriate organizational structure that reflects current needs. These issues are under constant review, and technologies including software agents are possible solutions.

NOTES

1 Eddie Obeng: www.pentaclethevbs.com.
2 www.landsend.com.
3 Matthew Higgins: www.firstdirect.com.
4 www.bt.com.

Key Concepts

As this text focuses on management issues surrounding virtual organization, this chapter discusses the concepts that underpin the changes in management thinking:

» the man–machine interface
» communities of practice
» trust
» self-organization
» the role of management.

"It is essential to release humanity from the false fixations of yesterday, which seem now to bind it to a rationale of action leading only to extinction."

Buckminster Fuller

The popular view of virtual organizations is that they are synonymous with virtual or *ad hoc* teams, and that they allow temporary alliances and greater flexibility than traditional organizations. An overriding conclusion is that computers have redefined the way we work, and in many cases the new arrangements are permanent, or at least long-term.

Research confirms that understanding virtual organizations is about understanding changes in management, new behavioral patterns, and new business models. These issues are far more important than the technology used. Discussion of virtual working has to take into account many influences: increasing numbers of part-time workers; more women at work; more self-employment; government regulation; and the move from an industrial to a service environment. Economic liberalization and globalization have demolished old assumptions and patterns of work are changing.

In this section we emphasize the management issues. There are a few well-known writers such as Lipnack and Stamps[1] and Eddie Obeng[2] (see Chapter 7) who are recognized as major contributors to the concept of virtual organizations. Here we start with a reminder of the man–machine dichotomy. A discussion of communities of practice is followed by consideration of trust and self-organization. A project studying the potential use of software agents is briefly reviewed, and the role of management examined.

MAN–MACHINE INTERFACE

Technological solutions abound.[3] Unfortunately, technology alone is not a solution.

Technology has changed both working practices and patterns of work. Organizations have become more flexible – hierarchical forms of management do not work in the new dynamic business world. Many organizations have become flatter; empowerment and delegation of responsibility is taking place. Yet truly cooperative, collaborative models of business are still rare. We need to apply systems thinking, but in a manner that allows appreciation of the human factors. There is still too much mechanistic thinking in management.

Charles Ehin[4] reminds us that we are talking teams, but still thinking the worker is a machine:

> "The management philosophy of the era of bathtub gin, gangsters, Model A Fords and the rise of General Motors was based on a machine metaphor. Refined at the turn of the century, by Frederick Taylor (scientific management), Henri Fayol (principles and elements of management), and Max Weber (bureaucracy), this is the management philosophy that still dominates our organizational landscape."

Rosenbrock[5] also discusses the difficulty of designing "a more humanly satisfactory technology" because that would contradict "the orthodox understanding of science, upon which our technology is based." He explains that industry is usually interpreted in terms of cause and effect, but sometimes it is based on purpose: such as meeting people's needs for satisfying work. People who incline to the first interpretation will favor automation and continue to treat people as machines; others will favor the subordination of machines to people.

COMMUNITIES OF PRACTICE

Although it is difficult for whole organizations to change to working in a virtual manner, it is clear that subdivisions have easily adapted. Design strategies for organizations have been evolving for many years. With the advent of information and communication technologies (ICT), including the Internet, communication between separate members of any organization has been revolutionized.

John Harney[6] suggests that in communities of practice the members, not outside authority, define what is important. They are "one manifestation of the tribal instinct in man," and they have always existed in some form. He quotes a story from Xerox where engineers formed a "Toolkit Working Group," reusing code from their original project to save time in later ones. Harney says that they are effective because they love what they are doing and the group is also about maintaining friendships. Now we need to recreate this way of working, using technology to aid communications regardless of location.

The potential to link distributed or mobile workforces through communications technologies has led to new ideas on managing the virtual team. Jones[7] has studied computer-mediated communication (CMC) and the social landscape. He is concerned with questions such as "Who are we when we are online?" He quotes Schuler:[8]

> "The old concept of community is obsolete in many ways and needs to be updated to meet today's challenges. The old or 'traditional' community was often exclusive, inflexible, isolated, unchanging, monolithic, and homogeneous. A new community – one that is fundamentally devoted to democratic problem-solving – needs to be fashioned from the remnants of the old."

Experiments on team working have a long history. Trist[9] published his thoughts on socio-technical systems in 1953. Herbst[10] presented the findings of "a new form of work organization, in which the team were given complete responsibility for the organization and performance of their task." In the late 1980s Digital Equipment UK experimented with high performance work systems,[11] and managers working there had to learn how to manage without authority.

Jessica Lipnack and Jeffrey Stamps[12] are acknowledged as experts in the study of virtual teams. They define a virtual team as:

> "a group of people who work interdependently with a shared purpose across space, time and organization boundaries using technology."

Quoting their work at Shell Oil Company, the reasons they give for choosing this way of working are:

» cost reduction;
» reduction of cycle time;
» increased innovation; and
» leveraged learning.

They suggest that this way of working should be part of a strategy, and that virtual teams provide strategic differentiation. They agree with many activists in the field that the traditional organization is becoming ''unglued'' – and redesigned using information technology. They also believe that most people will work in virtual teams in the coming decades. Working in the Information Age means that work is diffusing, reversing the move into towns that was a characteristic of the Industrial Revolution.

The four elements of virtual teams are people, purpose, links, and time. Organizations are process-based, input–output systems, and include many different types of team and degrees of virtuality, from the traditional work unit to global alliances. As Lipnack and Stamps soon found:

> ''Everything that goes wrong with in-the-same-place teams also plagues virtual teams – only worse.''

Tuckman's model[13] of team development (forming, storming, norming, performing) still applies! Many virtual teams waste time and money trying to get organized. Obeng has pointed out that we need to understand the full range of stakeholders. To use Lipnack's phrase, there will be ''rings of involvement'' – an extended team and external networks outside the core team.

TRUST

As all teams differ from each other, there is no prescription for implementation, but like many other practitioners, Lipnack and Stamps put great emphasis on building trust. They point out that we do not run our lives analytically, but we rely on trust, and this is even more important in virtual teams.

» The team cannot begin to work without trust.
» It's the ''grease'' that makes it work.
» Trust (or lack of it) is what people remember after the work is done.

A study on trust by Murray Clark[14] showed that any investigation of trust has to pay particular attention to the unit of analysis. Trust exists within individuals, within groups, between people, and between groups.

Much research effort is being expended on game theory, in the hope that this will contribute to the understanding of group dynamics. A much easier (and neglected) means of studying team behavior can be found in the Prisoners' Dilemma (sometimes known as the Red–Blue Game). Axelrod,[15] writing about reciprocal altruism, carried out many experiments with this game. The objective of the game is for both groups that are playing to end up with positive scores. The group with the higher positive score wins, but zero is not a positive score. When playing this with business people, it is hard to persuade them to adopt the win–win philosophy that is the key to success. There is always at least one player who wants to defeat the opposition. Richard Dawkins[16] describes the game in detail and produced a BBC Horizon film to illustrate the idea that "Nice Guys Finish First."

Reaching consensus and trust in any relationship takes time. It is actually surprisingly easy to gain an "online relationship," and often people are more open online than they would be when first meeting face-to-face. A factor that is hard to judge is the reliability of the person with whom you are dealing. A key factor in these situations is that the ground rules and specification of the work must be even more clearly defined in virtual working than in traditional teamwork. There is far less opportunity for revision and modification of the terms of reference as there are no *ad hoc* meetings at coffee breaks and meetings (real or through telecommunications) may be rare. There is often no knowledge of the members' track record. Trust is a necessary but insufficient condition.

SELF-ORGANIZATION

Perhaps because trust is a rare factor in business, self-organization is not greatly encouraged. Maybe also because it challenges the status quo and the security and power of senior managers. Another factor is that self-organization relies on self-discipline and makes responsibility transparent. It demands great self-knowledge. In the West, we are often exhorted to "Know Thyself." It is strange that it is rarely suggested that we do anything about what we find! Drucker[17] offers the advice:

"Do not try to change yourself – you are unlikely to succeed. Work to improve the way you perform."

A more interesting view was put forward by Pascale and Athos[18] in the following story:

> "One day a famous Japanese business executive paid a visit to a well-known Zen master to discuss Zen's relevance to management. Following Japanese etiquette, the master served green tea. When the cup of the visitor was full, the master kept pouring; the tea overflowed. The executive was startled. 'The cup is full; no more will go in.' Said the master, 'Like this cup, you are full of your own thoughts. How can I show you Zen unless you first empty your cup?'"

That story is now expressed by many of us as the idea of "unlearning." We have to unlearn our preconceptions about management, and then find new ways of using technology for groups. Much research centers on questions such as:

» improving task performance of work groups;
» overcoming space and time constraints on groups; and
» increasing access to information.[19]

Many would add the use of technology, both to reduce costs and to act as a control mechanism. Managers know about the use of technology for e-business, the integrated enterprise, and for automation of administrative work. They know about teleworking, video-conferencing, and other groupware technologies. The ability to monitor and audit every move of every employee has been paramount, leading to worries about "Big Brother" and invasion of privacy. The negative side of technology has been uppermost in everyone's mind. The idea of using technology to enhance self-organization and self-managed teams is less often discussed.

Ehin[20] states that we have become slaves of our own making to the point of refusing to question the nature of current structures. He suggests that people are not ignorant, but they cannot perceive new ideas:

> "it is very difficult to conceive what the world outside of your box looks like if you only have what amounts to a pinhole to see through to the outside world."

You cannot make people change, you need to encourage them by offering a role model and making it safe to experiment. In a recent research project[21] the author set up a series of workshops at 10 operational sites around the UK. The sponsoring company had a traditional command-and-control structure, but was attempting to find tools to aid teamwork and collaboration in an increasingly distributed workforce. It was also aware of the need to maintain the motivation of its employees in a dynamic marketplace.

Capture of field requirements can only be successful if input from the users is obtained. Despite the variety of structured methods for requirements analysis, most are designed for the use of software engineers. The latter are not always sympathetic to the needs of the business as they do not understand the unstructured way in which people generally work. Users are too often left out of the design stage, because of the difficulties of crossing functional boundaries, or even because the managers feel that only they should be involved. Too often, technical solutions are imposed from senior management.

Social contact is important for the staff in the research project. The automation of their work had resulted in resentment and the feeling of being small cogs in a large machine. Many traditional working practices had been eliminated. The project was designed to show that software agents could be used to mediate business activities. At the workshops, groups of 10 to 15 staff were introduced to the idea of collaborative software and agent technology. They were invited to discuss the ways in which this could be adapted to help their move towards self-managed teams. The idea of having ''electronic butlers'' negotiating deals on their behalf whilst they spent time on other work was well received at all levels. Managers could get rid of trivial work like allocating overtime. Other staff could save time on trying to make contact via telephone calls or waiting for information. Instead, it would be presented to them on their laptop next time they logged on.

Initially, the new software solution was presented as a means of ''bypassing'' the current operations management system. However, the research showed that trying to add on new features would destroy the integrity of that system. It also demonstrated the need to seek root causes and get rid of problems, rather than use technology to solve difficulties.

A particularly important finding was the clash of philosophies between the "push" of the traditional software systems (thus maintaining control by the management hierarchy) and the "pull" system encouraged by the new technologies. It became evident, when comparing this work with the systems in other organizations, that software systems already in place are one of the main factors preventing change. They were designed in the era of hierarchy and too often maintain "Old World" practices.

Using software agents as the basic elements of a self-organizing system, management would be reassured by the facility to monitor (if required); employees would have the freedom to organize their work in a manner that suited them, thus increasing job satisfaction and motivation. Allowing people to organize their work – trusting them to get the work done and not looking over their shoulder to control and dictate how it should be done – threatens our traditional view of management.

MANAGEMENT: WHAT VALUE DOES IT ADD?

Changes in business strategy and the development of new business models in turn lead to new ideas about the nature of management. Most organizations are focused on what they refer to as "value-added" operations. We now have to question the value of management itself. We need to shift our attention to every aspect of organization. If a company can now be based in cyberspace, why do we transfer our traditional (and often functional) ideas to that new way of working? When computers were first introduced into the workplace, they were used merely to computerize existing working practices. It was noticed that the enormous investment was not contributing very much to increased productivity. After some years, people began to automate processes rather than merely computerizing them. In a famous *Harvard Business Review* article, Hammer[22] suggested that we needed to rethink the way we worked.

Conservative thinking is still replicated in traditional organizational charts. Those charts show the hierarchical power structure of an organization. They depict management as a privilege and workers as a commodity. They miss out that most important link, the customer, and they do not show how the work gets done – the process flows.

Workers at the bottom of the hierarchy are expected to be doers rather than thinkers, so they must hang up their brains with their coats. To show the interdependence of all parts of an organization we need to think in terms of *process* hierarchy. (See Fig. 8.1.)

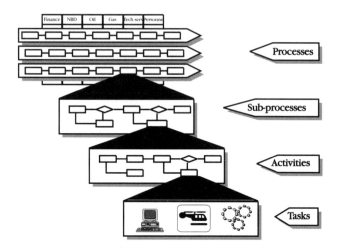

Fig. 8.1   Process hierarchy.

We need to organize to allow the work to get done. Deming said that people work in a system, and the job of the managers should be to improve the system with the help of the people working in it. What we are seeking now is a situation where technology is an enabler and a tool that aids new ways of working.

Ehin goes as far as to say we "must learn how to unmanage." He proposes that leaders should:

"Help develop a space where

» natural interaction or cooperation can take place without control
» there is self-reference, or form without structure.

Such a space allows minds to meet and true commitment and learning to flourish.''

How do you break the force of tradition? Previous experience can be the main reason that people do not listen to new ideas. Experience builds into values, and those values are rewarded. As Eddie Obeng emphasized, most organizations are designed so that learning is actually very effective. People learn a few things very effectively, then repeat them. The learning spreads out through the organization, and if you want to change it, you have to help people to unlearn and rebuild. Many cannot do that.

VIRTUAL WORKING: KEY MANAGEMENT ISSUES

» Unlearning.
» Trust.
» Commitment and collaboration.
» Listening to staff.
» Moving from hierarchical, bureaucratic command-and-control structures to outwardly focused, customer-service orientated organizations.
» Supporting people through change.
» Moving from "push" systems to structures that encourage self-organization.

NOTES

1 Lipnack, J. & Stamps, J. (2000) *Virtual Teams*. John Wiley & Sons. NB: They have now offered their work online as a tribute to the victims of September 11, (2001). See www.virtualteams.com.

2 Obeng, E. (1997) *New Rules for the New World*. Capstone.

3 See, for example, www.edocmagazine.com.

4 Ehin, C. (1993) "A high performance team is not a multi-part machine." *Journal of Quality and Participation*, December, pp. 11–21.

5 Rosenbrock, H. (1990) *Machines with a Purpose*. OUP.

6 Article found on www.edocmagazine.com/edoc_article.asp?ID = 22572.
7 Jones, S. (ed.) (1997) *Virtual Culture*. Sage.
8 Schuler, D. (1996) *New Community Networks*. ACM Press.
9 Trist, E.L. (1953) *Some Observations on the Machine Face as a Socio-technical System*. Tavistock Institute.
10 Herbst, P. (1962) *Autonomous Group Functioning*. Tavistock Institute.
11 For a case study see Buchanan, D. & McCalman, J. (1989) *High Performance Work Systems*. Routledge.
12 See Note 1.
13 See www.catalystonline.com/parts/thinking/tuckmans.html.
14 Personal communication, based on an internal report conducted for British Coal, August (1990).
15 Axelrod, R. (1984) *The Evolution of Co-operation*, Basic Books.
16 Dawkins, R. (1989) *The Selfish Gene*, OUP.
17 Drucker, P. (1999) "Managing oneself." *HBR*, March, pp. 65–74.
18 Pascale, R. & Athos, A. (1981) *The Art of Japanese Management*, Penguin.
19 See, for example, McGrath, J. & Hollingshead, A. (1994) *Groups Interacting with Technology*. Sage.
20 Ehin, C. (1995) "The ultimate advantage of self-organizing systems." *J. Quality and Participation*, September, pp. 30–38.
21 Collins, P. (1999) – the sponsoring company has requested anonymity.
22 Hammer, M. (1990) "Re-engineering work: Don't automate, obliterate." *HBR*, July–August, pp. 104–12.

Resources

Much has been written on the subject of virtual organizations. Books have been listed in the endnotes. Here, a representative sample of other references has been identified, including:

- » websites
- » trade associations
- » online journals
- » newsgroups.

If you are interested in working in a virtual organization, you will probably find this section irrelevant: you will have already discovered that your major resource is the Internet!

There is an amazing variety of material available. Once you start exploring, the scope of the subject seems to grow exponentially! The first thing to do is to define the boundaries of what you want to do. This will save frustrating searches on the Internet that do not produce fruitful sources or useful information. Each section contains a list of sources relevant to the issues discussed. Sites concerning your particular interest can be found via various search engines: www.google.com is very easy to use, but many people have their own favorites. www.worldbestwebsites.com/resources is another good starting point.

If you were hoping to find information about setting up your own online business, you could visit www.jasonrich.com for up-to-date advice. It is not the intention of this text to provide such detail.

PERSONAL NETWORKING

Much of the information in this text came from research and interviews with business colleagues. Personal networking is most definitely (and appropriately!) a great way to get information, and it is gratifying to find that so many people were interested and willing to share information and allowed publication of some of their work. If local friends and colleagues cannot provide the information you want, there are many online groups that welcome new members.

CONFERENCES

We hear so much about change. It's constant and it's dynamic. It is frustrating and challenging. We all need to take time out to think about the implications and to develop our strategies. An excellent way to do this is to attend conferences. Despite the plea of "I haven't got the time," it is well worth it. You are not trying to sell a pitch, and you can sit back and take stock. Recharge your batteries and your knowledge.

NEWSPAPERS AND BUSINESS JOURNALS

These are an essential part of your learning. Fortunately, many are now available online. *Harvard Business Review (HBR)*, *MIT Sloan Management Review (SMR)* and the *Californian Management Review (CMR)* are particularly useful sources of topical information. *Wired*, *Fortune*, *The Economist* and many others are easily obtainable. The Emerald Alert Service (email-admin@emeraldinsight.com) offers an online service, sending information about articles related to your chosen subjects. For a free trial, log on to http://www.emeraldinsight.com/rpsv/cgi-bin/emft/pl. *Business Week* and its archives are available at www.businessweek.com.

If you want regular updates of academic research, a good starting point would be www.virtual-organization.net. This is the site of Virtual Organization Net, which publishes the *Electronic Journal of Organizational Virtualness* (eJOV for short). Papers can be downloaded and cover a vast number of topics.

Conspectus is a useful publication for anyone interested in developments in information technology – see www.conspectus.com.

COMPANY WEBSITES

Online sources have been suggested within the text, and there are some general ones that are particularly useful. Some companies could not give permission to publish information for this text for company confidentiality reasons, but if you want case study material for specific companies, much is available on their Websites.

Many consultancy firms have good Websites. Some expect a payment for detailed papers, but many are free. If you subscribe to www.Gartner.com you can ask for a regular newsletter. The Butler Group also offers this service at opinionwire@butlergroup.com.

E-BUSINESS

Like all aspects of virtual organizations, the scope of virtual commerce is huge. Information on the Web is easy to find. If you log on to the Website of almost any company, you can now find information about their e-business. Cisco is actively encouraging all its suppliers and customers to use its Website and others will follow suit.

To learn about online auctions, try www.ebay.com for instance, and buy something online. Another site that "walks" you through the process is www.covisint.com – you do not need to be in the auto trade to use it, they offer a "test drive" to illustrate the power of the method. They also offer an insight into how the portal was designed, and share top tips on supply chain management. If you want more information, look up www.bizreport.com or search on sites such as www.europbestof.com. For information on navigating customer contact space, look at www.rockwell.com (or find it via www.callcentres.com.au). For collaborative planning, forecasting and replenishment (CPFR) there are details on www.cpfr.org and www.e-scrf.ac.uk. http://tli.isye.gatech.edu links you to the home page of Georgia Tech – one of the leading research centers in the USA. An excellent glossary can be found at http://www.tbg.co.uk/. MSI magazine has published a listing of leading business software vendors at www.manufacturingsystems.com/top100/.

UKCEB

The UK Council for Electronic Business – www.ukceb.org – is a not-for-profit organization that aims to help companies reorganize their business using appropriate technologies. They claim that the benefits of good e-business practice include:

» 10% increased turnover;
» informed decision-making;
» improved market share;
» faster response times; and
» increased customer satisfaction.

They have written a handbook on e-business, and are organizing a Practical Electronic Business Leadership Scheme (PeBLS). The aim is to help companies to assess their needs and to share best practice through networking and sharing of information. UKCeB list 18 key elements for full e-business, although the choice will depend on each organization's objectives.

TRADE ASSOCIATIONS AND PROFESSIONAL INSTITUTIONS

Very often your organization is a member of the appropriate body, and you are entitled to access to a variety of facilities. For example, the National Institute for Transport and Logistics (NITL) in Ireland publishes a list of useful sites in its journal, *Logistics Solutions*.

Cisco publish a regular "iQ Thought Leadership Newsletter" that can be sent by e-mail (contact iQ@cisco.com). You can also obtain more details from http://resources.cisco.com/app/tree.taf?asset_id=65323& section_id=4475.

For online human resource information, try www.business-intelligence.co.uk/reports/ehr/benefits.asp. Ironically, *Business Intelligence* is still publishing on CD-ROM and hard copy. www.hr.com is the largest web destination in North America if you believe their publicity. They can offer services such as online surveys. Basic information is free, but membership is mandatory after two visits.

NEWS GROUPS

News groups offer good reference material: BBC News Online http://news.bbc.co.uk/ is the Internet arm of the biggest broadcasting news-gatherer in the world. Agence France-Presse (www.afp.com) and Reuters (www.reuters.com) are other examples.

Specialist sites abound. There was no room for discussion of health services, but www.vh.org is an introduction to the virtual hospital – a digital health services library created at the University of Iowa. Another unusual find was www.serviceleader.org – the site for the Virtual Volunteering Project. The site aims to "encourage and assist in the development and success of volunteer activities."

For technical material, keep up to date with the BT Technology Journal – www.labs.bt.com/library/bttj/index.htm.

COMPANY INTRANETS

If you have a company intranet, you have a wonderful source of help. Quite apart from the Web pages, you have the opportunity to ask for help online. Companies such as Cisco have pages of frequently asked questions (FAQs). Many companies have chat rooms full of news. In one company a site was set aside for feedback, and staff could write their comments anonymously if they wished. That site gave more insights into the culture of the company than any other work. The "tone" of the messages gave away far more than the writers realized.

Many companies have information exchange pages: by posting problems on the Web, every member of staff can get help from anyone anywhere in the world. The kind of messages range from technical details to comments such as "the silence was stunning" from someone who obviously thought the response disappointing; to "my first reaction on reading this was 'don't even try'." Others request figures to help "sell" an idea to a partner, or ask for experience of specific situations. Trust that the information will be used in a correct manner is a key factor in such exchanges.

Several companies have issued laptops to their dispersed workforce so that such information can be shared. Many staff have not yet realized that there is so much information on hand. However, at the other extreme are company sites with millions of pages of information that give you "information overload." The important thing is to use your own firm's databases as a starting point.

ONLINE LEARNING

Web sites for e-learning include:

http://www.lamc.utexas.edu/fr/home/html

telnet://sol.uvic.ca6250

http://www.lamc.utexas.edu/fr/home/html

telnet://moo.syr.edu:7777/

http://www.parismatch.tm.fr/

www.utexas.edu

http://virtualsociety.sbc.ox.ac.uk

www.open.ac.uk

www.elearners.com

www.coe.uh.edu.insite/elec_pub/html1998/ts_mcin.html

www.21stnetwork.com/users/4588/

www.webster.comment.edu/hp/pages/darling/distance.html

www.online.uophx.edu

www.deta.gov.au/highered/eip-pubs/eip97-22/execsum.htm

www.homebusinesssolutions.com

www.cardean.com

www.athena.edu

http://www.cren.net/jbetc/jvb_cause.html

www.e-education.com

www.learndirect.com

www.avistar.com/education/education/html

www.yankeegroup.com

www.leeds.ac.uk/educcol/documents/000000669.html

www.lakewoodconferences.com/wp/ (overview of online learning)

www.cisco.com

www.srec.sreb.org/student/srecinfo/principles.html

Please note: Websites sometimes change their URL or are removed.

Guidelines to Going Virtual

Coping with the change to virtual working means you need to:

» look at the bigger picture;
» look at what you need to change about yourself;
» unlearn – replace old thinking with new ideas;
» develop new models;
» work out new rules;
» find fellow enthusiasts;
» act as a role model;
» redesign the business;
» have the courage to act; and
» have the courage to keep doing it.

"The trouble with the future is that it usually arrives before we are ready for it."

A.H. Glasgow

1. THE BIGGER PICTURE[1]

In 1988 Weatherall[2] wrote:

"a somewhat coldly analytical attitude to the existing operation of the business is recommended ... departments can actually be disbanded (or combined); their objectives or means of operation can, and sometimes should be, radically changed."

Has your organization been brave enough to embrace such radical change?

Going virtual is not about technology. It is about changing the way we manage our organizations. You may talk of self-managed teams and self-organization, or the changes may be labeled as "empowerment." The labels do not matter. We have to learn to give both authority and responsibility to employees to allow them to act in a way that improves the way the work is done. This has to be done to provide levels of customer service way beyond anything we have been used to. Customer expectations have changed, and that factor alone is sufficient to force the issue onto your agenda. "Business as usual" has become obsolete. It is no longer a matter of "whether to go virtual" but "to what extent and how?"

Managers need help in deciding how to go about achieving their objectives, and getting started is very difficult. Markides[3] includes a very interesting discussion on "How to escape mental models," and points out that too often, mental models allow us to think passively, or perhaps not at all. He reminds us that people:

"tend to reject new information that contradicts what they already believe."

2. HAVE YOU GOT WHAT IT TAKES?

That is a key question. Are you sufficiently motivated to try something new? Are you willing to grasp unexpected opportunities? Are you open to new ideas?

Adopting a virtual way of working is not about how much technology you have, but about how you really want to work and what experience you wish to offer to customers. How can you improve operations management within your organization? Are there better ways to invest in resources with the ability to delight customers? What is needed is thinking that promotes better relationships, both internally and externally.

It has been stated that the ability to recruit, train, motivate, and retain high quality staff was the most important challenge facing organizations. Providing an enjoyable working experience for our staff is as important as developing systems and processes that speed up and facilitate communications with customers. New technology will automate yet more of the routine tasks, but those developments must be balanced with the need to provide user-friendly interfaces.

Management issues will continue to dominate as it is more widely recognized that people issues are more important than either technical or economic concerns. It used to be said, "Quality is free." That is still true to the extent that good quality means that you have cut out wasteful practices; you have streamlined your processes and technology to make them customer-facing; and you have empowered your staff to make decisions. By removing layers of management, and building an atmosphere of trust, you energize your staff and make their work more worthwhile.

3. COPING WITH CHANGE

Coping with change can feel like being at the center of an earthquake.[4] Those around you will feel the aftershocks for a considerable time. Managers may find it so hard to cope with change that they cannot help colleagues to manage the uncertainty they feel. The structure of change can be summarized in three phases:

» the ending of the old order;
» transition; and
» consolidation and new beginnings.

In the first phase people might understand intellectually, but not accept what is happening emotionally. They might go through several stages on the way to full acceptance:

» shock
» denial
» incompetence/uncertainty
» gradual acceptance/letting go of the past
» testing
» search for meaning
» integration and increased confidence.

It takes time for the idea of constant change and new ways of working to become second nature. Organizations have to provide appropriate resources to support their employees through transition. Managing such relationships, both internally and with external partners, is a critical factor in developing virtual organizations. Those that ignore the feelings of loss and fear will fail to survive.

4. MANAGING CHANGE

Managers in large companies have suggested that change management is a very messy business. Textbook methods tend to be very systematic in their approach, with "10 Steps" or "Three Stages" or however many elements the writer wishes to include. Such methods give a level of reassurance, as they imply that if you get them right, you will achieve the goals you have set yourself. It is useful to carry out systematic reviews of resources, the functions of the organization, and systems. Such a "project management" approach works well with things. Change management is about *people*.

Going virtual might be state-of-the-art, but many of the techniques to get you there have evolved from tried and tested quality principles. Total Quality Management (TQM) and Continuous Improvement (CI) have been regarded as "projects" rather than as a journey towards business excellence. Root cause analysis and process mapping are basic techniques, but remain key to the understanding and implementation of change. Facilitators still have a role to play. One of the main differences is that you can no longer afford to let improvement teams work out the changes at their own tempo. Time targets have to be set and a greater sense of urgency is required.

There are three elements to managing change:

» management style;
» culture; and
» environment.

Style influences culture; culture influences the environment, which in turn influences attitudes and behavior. What we are seeking is not just a change in the way we use technology, but change in behavior. This involves training people; integrating with them; removing the "them and us" barriers; and developing trust. Slogans and exhortations just do not work. Managers have to initiate actions that will change perceptions of their role in the organization. They must act as catalysts and "walk the talk" themselves. The philosophy can be summed up as a culture of working together and sharing knowledge. (See Fig. 10.1.)

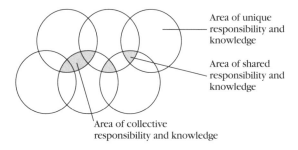

Fig. 10.1 Working together and sharing knowledge.

5. LEARN NEW RULES

Charles Handy[5] recognized the paradoxes we have to cope with. He tried to include a sense of purpose in the way we work. Noting that:

"The world is up for reinvention in so many ways. Creativity is born in chaos. What we do, what we belong to, why we do it,

when we do it, where we do it – these may all be different and
they could be better."

Handy challenges us:

"We cannot wait for great visions from great people, for they are
in short supply at the end of history. It is up to us to light our own
small fires in the darkness."

Be prepared to "unlearn" and invest in lifelong learning. Increase your
level of computer literacy, and try out virtual working for yourself
if you have not yet done so. Find new mental models that involve
interdependencies between both functions and separate parts of the
organization. Try a processual management model that integrates all
facets of your organization. (See Fig. 10.2.)

6. BE A ROLE MODEL

The starting point is very personal: you have to believe in the change
yourself and become a role model. You also need to keep in mind
when you are involved in change management that it is a team effort.
A traditional, bureaucratic hierarchy will not work. The key now is
to become a coach/leader/facilitator, which may mean that you are
deliberately working yourself out of a job – not an easy situation for
most of us to contemplate.

Eddie Obeng recommends that you push on open doors: convert
those who are ready to change. Turning around the whole organization
is like moving an ocean liner: it is a very slow process. Better to form
a small group to act as catalysts by leading the way and demonstrating
not only that it is possible, but also showing the potential of new ways
of working.

In Shell, for example, they have a network of employees who play
different roles. You will not find them on an organization chart, as many
only come together for a specific project. Understanding how difficult
it is to describe and support change, the company relies on a mixture
of change agent specialists, support staff, and internal "consultants,"
all linked to human resource specialists who are seen as partners in the
process. They still use external consultants in the traditional manner,

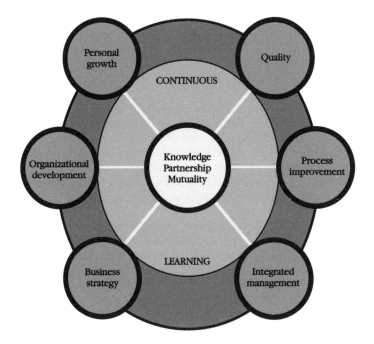

Fig. 10.2 Processual management.

but rely heavily on their "virtual network" of internal staff all around the globe. They have discovered that you cannot make things work by having a group or department "in charge." The ideas have to be assimilated across the company, with local champions backed up by specialist staff.

7. WHITHER MANAGEMENT?

The challenge to many organizations is that senior management is middle-aged, middle-class, male, and conventional. Success stories such as the transformation of Dell, IBM, and Cisco demonstrate that major change is achievable, but it is also clear that younger staff often wish to move faster than their bosses. They are more willing to accept "unconventional" ways of working and to experiment with new business models. Many years ago, Rosabeth Moss Kanter[6] suggested that success in business was beginning "to look like a feat for magicians." She stressed the need for big companies to become more entrepreneurial:

> "Even though companies have been exhorted to ... combine cost control in the name of efficiency with investment in pursuit of innovation – for the most part there has been a tendency to emphasize one or the other end of the spectrum ... the ultimate corporate balancing act (is to) cut back and grow. Trim down and build. Accomplish more, and do it in new areas, with fewer resources ... Can the elephants start learning to dance?"

It is clear that some companies have indeed learned to dance. A senior businessman in a major logistics company summarized it as "five laws." There are huge opportunities if you are willing to:

» be unconventional, different, and quick;
» focus totally on the customer;
» develop partnerships with customers and suppliers;
» abandon your baggage; and
» cultivate your heritage.

How do you blend all this together? The hope was expressed that the Millennium would usher in a new workplace: "productive, profitable and inclusive, where respect and dignity for the members/workers is part of business as usual." Many workers do not yet feel that this has been achieved. Whilst senior managers are developing their strategies, they must involve their staff at all levels. This will entail a massive culture change and shift in managerial attitudes. Evidence from current work suggests that it is happening – but very slowly.

8. A STRATEGY FOR GOING VIRTUAL

It is essential to develop a strategy for "going virtual." This thinking must start at the highest level of management, as it complements the corporate strategy of the organization. Each organization has to define its needs: it will be rare to find a company that is entirely virtual, just as it is rare nowadays to find an organization with no elements of virtual working.

It is important to decide the scale of the change you wish to implement. To cope with large-scale projects the "chunk it" philosophy is a wise one. The scope of the implementation in any organization will depend on the drivers that apply in a particular sector. They may be:

» markets;
» global economics;
» competitors;
» government or international regulations; or
» technological developments.

Implementation is a process, and these five drivers tend to merge into a set of mutually reinforcing forces. Corporations have discovered that they must adopt more entrepreneurial cultures and that becoming agile and flexible is an integral part of their survival strategy. Using technologies to "go virtual" is one way of achieving these competencies.

Michael Porter[7] has recently published an interesting contribution to this debate. He writes:

"Ultimately, strategies that integrate the Internet and traditional competitive advantages and ways of competing should win in many industries."

He suggests that the "new economy" of the dotcom world is an irrelevant phrase, and that the "old economy" is merging so quickly with the "new" that

"soon it will be difficult to distinguish them ... While a new means of conducting business has become available, the fundamentals of competition remain unchanged."

There is certainly no prescription for that "new means of conducting business," although you can develop "rules" or a structure to aid the change. If your organization is global, you will have to learn to change behaviors, attitudes, and mindsets. You will have to embrace and manage diversity. It is an enormous challenge.

9. DO IT

Many new enterprises have sprung up and have challenged the giants. Doing more of what you did will just get you more of what you got. Your strategy has to embrace new business models and new ways of working. This is not something that can be left to middle managers or to one function such as the human resources department. Senior management has a duty to take a bird's-eye view of the total environment and position their organization for the long term. As the Internet is here to stay, that means having an Internet strategy. Your competitors are going virtual; your customers are expecting ever-higher standards of delivery and communication; and both are utilizing an increasing variety of technological solutions. You must therefore choose which is most suitable for you.

10. DO IT AGAIN

Do what is right for you. You do not have to copy a model from another company. There is no prescription. There is no "one model fits all." How you use technology to become virtual or to increase your networking depends on your company strategy. Do what fits your own organizational goals and aspirations.

Much of what is required is common to any large project: cost, quality and time are important factors, and balancing the three factors demands involvement and commitment from senior management.

Many companies fail in their efforts because they underestimate the "people" factors. Going virtual is 10% technology, 30% process, and 60% people.

Many years ago, Mary Parker Follett[8] stated:

> "The important thing about responsibility is not to whom you are responsible, but for what you are responsible."

As motivation increases, staff loyalty grows and attrition rates decrease. In turn, customer service levels increase and customer retention and loyalty grow. The aim must be to create this virtuous circle in our virtual world of multimedia virtual organizations and networks.

TEN STEPS TO GOING VIRTUAL

Coping with the change to virtual working means you need to follow these steps.

1 Look at the bigger picture.
2 Look at what you need to change about yourself.
3 Unlearn – replace old thinking with new ideas.
4 Develop new models.
5 Work out new rules.
6 Find fellow enthusiasts.
7 Act as a role model.
8 Redesign the business.
9 Have the courage to act.
10 Have the courage to keep doing it.

NOTES

1 This chapter is based on both my own research and my discussions with Eddie Obeng. When we met, we talked about the difficulties of implementing change. Too often people think they can tick off a checklist and thus achieve their goals. This is a list of guiding principles, not a checklist.
2 Weatherall, A. (1988) *CIM: From Fundamentals to Implementation*. Butterworths.
3 Markides, C. (2000) *All the Right Moves*. Harvard Business School Press.
4 Material from interviews at Royal SunAlliance (UK).
5 Handy, C. (1994) *The Empty Raincoat*. Hutchinson.
6 Moss Kanter, R. (1989) *When Giants Learn to Dance*. Unwin.
7 Porter, M. (2000) "*Strategy and the Internet*." *HBR*, March, pp. 63–78.
8 Follett, M.P. (1949) *Freedom and Co-ordination*. Management Publications Trust.

Frequently Asked Questions (FAQs)

Q1: What are the benefits of going virtual?

A: See Chapters 1 and 7.

Q2: What is the difference between virtual organizations and networks?

A: See Chapter 2.

Q3: Is this the same as virtual reality?

A: See Chapter 6.

Q4: Do I need to know about telecommunications to understand virtual organizations?

A: See Chapter 2.

Q5: What are the basic concepts of virtual organizations?

A: See Chapters 2 and 3.

Q6: In what ways does management thinking affect the implementation of virtual organization?

A: See Chapters 3, 8, and 10.

Q7: What is disintermediation? Is this the same as self-service?

A: See Chapter 4.

Q8: Do you mean the virtual university?

A: See Chapter 4.

Q9: Is this all about the global village?

A: See Chapter 5.

Q10: How is this linked to e-business?

A: See Chapter 5.

Q11: Will there be changes when new technologies are developed?

A: See Chapter 6.

Q12: Do virtual organizations work?

A: See Chapter 7.

Q13: Will this model be suitable for my sector of industry?

A: See Chapters 4, 5, and 7.

Q14: What do I need to understand before I can go virtual?

A: See Chapters 2, 3, and 8.

Q15: Where can I get help?

A: See Chapter 9.

Q16: How do I start?

A: See Chapter 10.

Acknowledgments

I owe many thanks to my business friends and colleagues who have contributed so much: Steve Spreckley, John Pimblott, Brian Plowman, John Foster, Matthew Higgins, Nick Bacon, John Shepherdson, Tom Richardson, Sam Brown, Bert Kolz, Justin Urquart Stewart, Laura McKee, Jamie Clyde, Nicky Kibble, Malcolm Diamond, and Roy Leitch. Derek Wood deserves a particular mention for his sponsorship of my original research at Digital Equipment UK Ltd. My students have made an invaluable contribution, by challenging and discussing the issues. Andreas Hronopoulos carried out some of the research for online recruitment. Thank you Eddie Obeng for such an interesting and fun interview!

Suzy Mayhew of Access Conferences International has been of special assistance, as she has allowed me to attend relevant conferences to upgrade my knowledge. The caliber of their speakers has been excellent, and several of those speakers have kindly contributed to this text. Attendance at conferences and workshops has been partly sponsored by the Institute of Management Services. David Charlton and Jan Smith, editors of the Institute's journal *Management Services*, deserve a special thank you for their support over many years.

Index